WITHDRAWAL

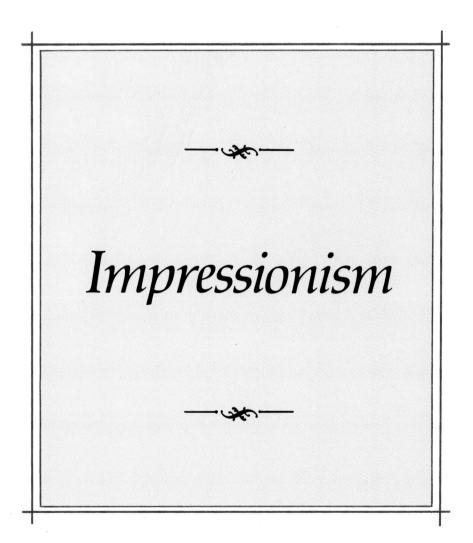

Impressionism

GREAT ARTISTS OF THE WESTERN WORLD

Impressionism

Edouard Manet

—❧—

Edgar Degas

—❧—

Claude Monet

—❧—

Pierre–Auguste Renoir

MARSHALL CAVENDISH · LONDON · NEW YORK · SYDNEY

Staff Credits

Editors	Clive Gregory LL B Sue Lyon BA (Honours)	**Picture Researchers**	Vanessa Fletcher BA (Honours) Flavia Howard BA (Honours) Jessica Johnson BA
Art Editors	Kate Sprawson BA (Honours) Keith Vollans LSIAD		
Deputy Editor	John Kirkwood B Sc (Honours)	**Production Controllers**	Steve Roberts Alan Stewart BSc
Sub-editors	Caroline Bugler BA (Honours), MA Sue Churchill BA (Honours) Alison Cole BA, M Phil Jenny Mohammadi Nigel Rodgers BA (Honours), MA Penny Smith Will Steeds BA (Honours), MA	**Secretary**	Lynn Smail
		Publisher	Terry Waters Grad IOP
		Editorial Director	Maggi McCormick
		Production Executive	Robert Paulley B Sc
		Consultant and Authenticator	Sharon Fermor BA (Honours) Lecturer in the Extra-Mural Department of London University and Lecturer in Art History at Sussex University
Designers	Stuart John Julie Stanniland		

Reference Edition 2001

Marshall Cavendish Corporation
99 White Plains Road
Tarrytown, NY 10591-9001

Printed in Malaysia

All rights reserved. No part of this book may be reproduced or utilized in any form or by any means electronic or mechanical including photocopying, recording, or by any information storage and retrieval system, without prior written permission from the publisher and copyright holder.

© *Marshall Cavendish Limited 1987*

Library of Congress Cataloging-in-Publication Data

Great Artists of the Western World.

 Includes index.
 1. Artists—Biography. I. Marshall Cavendish Corporation
N40.G77 1987 709'.2'2 [B] 86—23863

ISBN 0-86307-743-9 (set)
 0-86307-750-1 (vol. 7)

Preface

Looking at pictures can be one of the greatest pleasures that life has to offer. Note, however, those two words 'can be'; all too many of us remember all too clearly those grim afternoons of childhood when we were dragged, bored to tears and complaining bitterly, through room after room of Italian primitives by well-meaning relations or tight-lipped teachers. It was enough to put one off pictures for life – which, for some of us, was exactly what it did.

For if gallery-going is to be the fun it should be, certain conditions must be fulfilled. First, the pictures we are to see must be good pictures. Not necessarily great pictures – even a few of these can be daunting, while too many at a time may prove dangerously indigestible. But they must be well-painted, by good artists who know precisely both the effect they want to achieve and how best to achieve it. Second, we must limit ourselves as to quantity. Three rooms – four at the most – of the average gallery are more than enough for one day, and for best results we should always leave while we are still fresh, well before satiety sets in. Now I am well aware that this is a counsel of perfection: sometimes, in the case of a visiting exhibition or, perhaps, when we are in a foreign city with only a day to spare, we shall have no choice but to grit our teeth and stagger on to the end. But we shall not enjoy ourselves quite so much, nor will the pictures remain so long or so clearly in our memory.

The third condition is all-important: we must know something about the painters whose work we are looking at. And this is where this magnificent series of volumes – one of which you now hold in your hands – can make all the difference. No painting is an island: it must, if it is to be worth a moment's attention, express something of the personality of its painter. And that painter, however individual a genius, cannot but reflect the country, style and period, together with the views and attitudes of the people among whom he or she was born and bred. Even a superficial understanding of these things will illuminate a painting for us far better than any number of spotlights, and if in addition we have learnt something about the artist as a person – life and loves, character and beliefs, friends and patrons, and the places to which he or she travelled – the interest and pleasure that the work will give us will be multiplied a hundredfold.

Great Artists of the Western World will provide you with just such an insight into the life and work of some of the outstanding painters of Europe and America. The text is informative without ever becoming dry or academic, not limiting itself to the usual potted biographies but forever branching out into the contemporary world outside and beyond workshop or studio. The illustrations, in colour throughout, have been dispensed in almost reckless profusion. For those who, like me, revel in playing the Attribution Game – the object of which is to guess the painter of each picture before allowing one's eye to drop to the label – the little sections on 'Trademarks' are a particularly happy feature; but every aficionado will have particular preferences, and I doubt whether there is an art historian alive, however distinguished, who would not find some fascinating nugget of previously unknown information among the pages that follow.

This series, however, is not intended for art historians. It is designed for ordinary people like you and me – and for our older children – who are fully aware that the art galleries of the world constitute a virtually bottomless mine of potential enjoyment, and who are determined to extract as much benefit and advantage from it as they possibly can. All the volumes in this collection will enable us to do just that, expanding our knowledge not only of art itself but also of history, religion, mythology, philosophy, fashion, interior decoration, social customs and a thousand other subjects as well. So let us not simply leave them around, flipping idly through a few of their pages once in a while. Let us read them as they deserve to be read – and welcome a new dimension in our lives.

John Julius Norwich is a writer and broadcaster who has written histories of Venice and of Norman Sicily as well as several works on history, art and architecture. He has also made over twenty documentary films for television, including the recent Treasure Houses of Britain series which was widely acclaimed after repeated showings in the United States.

Lord Norwich is Chairman of the Venice in Peril Fund, and member of the Executive Committee of the British National Trust, an independently funded body established for the protection of places of historic interest and natural beauty.

John Julius Norwich

Contents

Introduction

Impressionism is regarded by many as the cradle of modern art. The innovations which it brought represented a genuine break with Academic tradition and sowed the seeds of many 20th-century developments in painting.

One of the most important factors contributing to the rise of the movement was the loosening of the stranglehold which the Salons had on French art. Since their inception, these official exhibitions had been the benchmark by which a painter could measure his success. Over the years, this convention, which favoured the more conservative artists, had occasionally been challenged.

Hitherto, such protests had always been made by individuals and had barely threatened the standing of the Salon. However, in 1863, the backlash from a particularly vociferous group of rejected artists persuaded Emperor Napoleon III to institute a 'Salon des Refusés' (p.14), where their works could be shown. The painters involved in this exhibition included Manet, Whistler and Pissarro and, while the public reaction was predictably derisive, the principle of a group exhibiting away from the confines of the Salon had been established. This set an important precedent for the Impressionist exhibitions, which were to begin a decade later.

The Gentleman Artist
The most controversial painting to be seen at the Salon des Refusés was The Luncheon on the Grass (pp.24-5) and the furore which it aroused helped to push Edouard Manet to the fore of the Parisian avant-garde. He shied away from this responsibility, as he was in later years to shy away from the Impressionists, preferring to follow his own artistic course.

In fact, most of Manet's greatest paintings could more accurately be described as Realist rather than Impressionist. In this, he was largely influenced by his friendship with two distinguished writers, the novelist Zola (p.30) and the poet Baudelaire. Manet met the latter in 1858 and responded enthusiastically to Baudelaire's art criticism and, in particular, to his call for painters to depict modern life, rather than dwell on the past.

The Concert in the Tuileries Gardens (pp.12-13), with its bustling crowd, was a clear result of this, while, in his two most controversial paintings, Manet tried to re-cast traditional models in a novel mould. Both The Luncheon on the Grass (pp.24-5) and Olympia (pp.26-7) were based on

Renaissance compositions, but shocked contemporaries by the modern context in which they were placed.

In essence, Manet's work was amoral rather than immoral and, in this respect, he was followed by the other Impressionists. In his wake, the group's corporate style grew out of the Realist movement. Hitherto, in the mainstream of French painting, artists had been expected to marry an excellence of technique and truth to nature with a high level of moral, intellectual or emotional content. But, by the 1870s, these two paths were beginning to diverge, with the Impressionists concentrating on the purely visual aspects of art, while the Symbolist painters maintained the importance of its subject-matter. These two strands were later to be reunited by the Post-Impressionists.

Where the Impressionists differed from the Realists was in their emphasis on technique. What the former observed was, in general, less important than the manner in which it was portrayed. In Manet's case, this was affected by two main factors. His interest in Japanese woodblock prints led him to flatten his forms and heighten his colours and he was hugely influenced by the Spanish paintings from the Orléans collection, which he was able to see after their confiscation in 1848. Manet remained an experimental artist, however, and, largely through the encouragement of Berthe Morisot, he adopted plein air painting late in his career, producing a number of typically Impressionist boating scenes, for example, pp.20-21.

The Fleeting Impression
Despite his long struggle for public recognition, Manet's talent was swiftly acclaimed by a select band of writers and artists. In addition to the praise of Zola and Baudelaire, he was hailed as a pioneer by the group which met at the Café Guerbois. Among his new acolytes here was the young Monet. Along with Pissarro, Monet epitomizes most closely the values of Impressionism and he remained devoted to the movement.

Monet's mature style was based on the fundamental doctrine of Impressionism – the practice of open-air painting. Naturally, there had been precedents for this. Many landscapists used to sketch outdoors, although the composition and execution of their finished pictures were invariably undertaken inside the studio.

The formation of Monet's style, however, came

would be hard to overestimate the contribution made by these two artists to the emergence of the Impressionist movement. Boudin, in particular, anticipated several of its most salient features. By the 1850s, for example, he had developed the habit of noting down the date, time of day and prevailing wind on all his studies of the Normandy coastline. This concern with the precise conditions under which a painting was executed was typical of the systematic approach adopted by the Impressionists.

Capturing Light
The rationale behind painting in the open air was, in fact, a purely scientific one. The study of optics had made great strides in the 19th century and one of its main discoveries indicated that the colour of any specific object was not inherent in the object itself, but was determined by the ever-changing

The artists
(from top) Monet at 35, in a portrait by Renoir; Renoir in 1875, when he was living in Paris; Degas at 30; Manet in 1867, aged 35.

Manet's natural light
(right) In this picture – Argenteuil – Manet tried to show the effects of light as he saw them. He painted the scene in patches of bright colour.

from two more immediate sources. He benefited from his spell in Gleyre's studio, where he met the nucleus of the Impressionist group – Renoir, Sisley and Bazille. In addition, Gleyre, despite the glacial Classicism of his pictures, was a surprisingly progressive teacher, who actively encouraged his pupils to paint out of doors.

Even more important to Monet, though, was the influence of Boudin and Jongkind, with whom he worked during his stay at Le Havre in 1862. It

reflections of light from it. As a result, the idea of painting a landscape in a studio, either from memory or from sketches, appeared quite inadequate to the Impressionists. For them, a painter had to work outdoors because he was seeking to capture the effect of light itself, rather than just form or colour.

Obviously, painting in the open air presented certain practical problems, since light conditions could alter so rapidly. Sargent, for example, would only work on his plein air paintings at a set time of the day, but most of the Impressionists found this unacceptable and elected, instead, to employ speedier painting methods.

In most cases, they relied on the optical mixture that could be obtained by juxtapozing complementary colours. This technique was derived from the scientific writings of Eugène Chevreul, whose theories had been known to Delacroix earlier in the century. Through it, a painting might look sketchy at close quarters, but would assume genuine form from a greater distance. It was this 'unfinished' look which the critics of both Delacroix and the Impressionists found so objectionable.

The Art of Pleasure

Monet's experiments with light and open-air painting were not taken up by all the Impressionists (they played a relatively small part, for example, in the work of Degas and Manet) but they certainly inspired Renoir. For him, though, landscape was less important and his exploration of light effects was largely confined to figure compositions like The Swing (p.116).

However, while Renoir's style – at least in his early pictures – resembled that of Monet, his choice of subject-matter was much closer to Manet. His most engaging paintings are those portraying modern Parisian life and, in this respect, works like the Luncheon of the Boating Party (pp.124-5) and Le Moulin de la Galette (pp.114-15) are direct descendents of the Concert in the Tuileries Gardens (pp.12-13). But, where Manet's picture is notable for its elegant sense of detachment, Renoir's works convey an irresistible warmth and friendliness. Pleasure and the joys of life was at the core of his art, outweighing any commitment he may have felt to the theoretical values of the Impressionist movement.

Like several other members of the group, Renoir soon began to question the direction he was taking. His acceptance at the 1878 Salon decided him

against contributing to the next three Impressionist exhibitions (1879-81) and his doubts increased after his travels in 1881, which prompted him to adopt a more classical style (see The Bathers, p.114).

Portraits of Paris

Degas, too, had reservations about the Impressionists. Even though he exhibited at all but one of their shows, he vehemently refused to accept that he was one of their number and, indeed, his art did run counter to some of the most fundamental tenets of the group. He did not paint in the open air, preferring the discipline of studio work. Nor was he especially interested in the interplay of light and colour within nature. Instead his art revolved around the study of the human form.

Where Degas shared the most common ground with other Impressionists was in the modernity and the immediacy of his subject-matter. After his uncertain, academic beginnings, Degas launched into the portrayal of contemporary Parisian life with enthusiasm. In his groups of paintings on dancers, washerwomen or racing, he explored his respective themes as exhaustively as Monet had done in his landscape series.

Both artists were, effectively, pursuing the same end – that of capturing an instant in time on canvas. In Monet's case, this required careful observation of specific light effects while, for Degas, it entailed a radically new approach to composition. In place of the clarity and order that would normally be found in most pictures, Degas sought an irregularity that might initially look clumsy, but which was truer to nature. He employed a revolutionary 'snapshot' technique to achieve this aim, zeroing in close to the action and frequently cutting off heads or arms at the edges of his picture surface (The Opéra Orchestra, p.57, is a typically daring example of this). Degas was assisted in this by the use of photographs, even though his ability to capture a specific movement or gesture was unparalleled. The disconsolate gaze of his absinthe drinker (p.62), for example, appears so natural that it is hard to believe that the picture was composed in the studio.

The eighth and final Impressionist exhibition was held in 1886, with the battle for recognition largely won. Monet, Renoir and Degas were finally managing to sell their works successfully and the movement that was to affect virtually every branch of modern art continued to gain momentum.

Manet

1832-1883

Edouard Manet was one of the most original and influential painters of the 19th century. His unconventional scenes from modern life and his breathtakingly bold brushwork brought new life to French painting and were an inspiration to the Impressionists. But Manet did not see himself as a revolutionary; indeed, he always thought of himself as following in the footsteps of the Old Masters.

The critics thought otherwise, and subjected Manet to unprecedented abuse, condemning his work as incompetent and, in the case of his nudes, obscene. Although he had no need to earn his living by painting, because he came from a wealthy family, the harsh criticism hurt him deeply. Manet longed for recognition, but he was denied all public honours until late in life, when he was crippled by illness.

11

The Unlikely Revolutionary

A gentleman artist, always impeccably turned-out, Manet was completely unprepared for the scandal his paintings provoked. And he was continually surprised by his own lack of success.

Edouard Manet was born in Paris on 23 January 1832, the eldest son of a senior civil servant in the Ministry of Justice. With this comfortable, upper middle-class background, Edouard was destined – in his father's eyes, at least – for a safe legal career.

Edouard, however, had neither the temperament nor the inclination to follow in his father's footsteps. From the beginning he found school dull and was consistently inattentive – he much preferred his home life, where he could be with his mother, Eugénie, whom he adored. A woman of artistic inclinations, she loved music and arranged for Edouard and his two younger brothers to take piano lessons. In the evenings, Edouard also learned to draw, under the guidance of his uncle, Edmond Fournier, who had a passion for art.

By 1848, when Edouard was 16, matters between himself and his father came to a head. Edouard was expected to go to law school, but by now he was determined to become a painter. M. Manet was outraged by this suggestion, but eventually father and son reached a compromise:

Edouard agreed to enter the Navy rather than become a lawyer or a painter. He promptly failed his entrance exams, but was given the chance to retake them if he spent six months as an apprentice on a transport ship. On 9 December 1848, Manet set sail for Rio de Janeiro.

A CAREER AS A PAINTER

On his return, Manet resat his exams and failed yet again. He had learned that the hardships of life at sea were not for him and begged his father to allow him to become a painter. Recognizing his son's seriousness, M. Manet relented, and in January, 1850, Manet enrolled at the Paris studio of the respected figure painter Thomas Couture.

Manet's talent as a painter was instinctive and he very quickly showed greater promise than any of his fellow students. But at 18, he already had decided ideas about painting, and for the most part these were not his master's. The outworn traditions and the artificiality of academic art

A fashionable gathering
(below) Manet adored Parisian society, and his painting of a Concert in the Tuileries Gardens *(1862) shows the world he moved in. Mingling with the dandies and fashionable ladies are some of his gifted contemporaries – the composer, Jacques Offenbach, the writer, Théophile Gautier, and the poet, Charles Baudelaire. Manet's brother, Eugène, is prominent in the centre of the composition and Manet himself appears on the extreme left.*

Key Dates

1832 born in Paris

1848 joins the navy

1850 enrols at Couture's studio

1860 rents studio in Batignolles quarter

1862 father dies; large inheritance

1863 marries Suzanne Leenhoff. Exhibits *The Luncheon on the Grass* at the Salon des Refusés.

1865 *Olympia* provokes a scandal

1868 meets Berthe Morisot

1869 frequents the Café Guerbois

1874 paints with Monet at Argenteuil

1879 onset of fatal illness

1881 awarded the Légion d'Honneur

1883 dies in Paris

Jean-Loup Charmet

The perfect gentleman
Manet was elegant, cultured and urbane. Described by Zola as a man of 'exquisite politeness' and 'extreme amiability', he was a rebel only in his art.

Manet/Musée d'Orsay, Paris

M. and Mme Auguste Manet
*(left) Manet's parents were wealthy and
highly respected. His father was a stern
and self-righteous man, who expected
his son to pursue a career in the civil
service, similar to his own. His mother,
on the other hand, was an artistic woman
who loved music. Manet was always
extremely close to her.*

Bibliothèque Nationale

Wife and 'godson'
*(left and below) When he
was 18, Manet fell in love
with his 20-year-old piano
teacher, Suzanne
Leenhoff. They married in
1863, and an 11-year-old
boy, Léon-Edouard Koëlla,
was a special guest at
their wedding. Léon was
introduced as Suzanne's
younger brother and
Manet's godson. But it
seems certain that he was
the couple's son – born on
29 January 1852.*

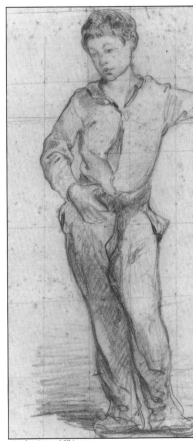

Art Institute of Chicago

National Gallery, London

exasperated him. When he was given a plaster cast
of an antique statue to copy, he drew it upside
down – because it was 'more interesting' that way.
'You've got to belong to your own period', he said,
'and paint what you see'.

During these years at Couture's studio, Manet
presented an image that was to change little as he
grew older. He was an attractive man, of medium
height and strong physique. His mouth, turned up
at the corners, was ironic. His glance was keen; his
eyes were deepset but very mobile and he walked
with an elegant swagger. Manet was urbane and
charming – in fact, an unlikely revolutionary. In
spite of his unconventional ideas on painting, he
wanted above all to be accepted by the Salon, the
established centre of the French artistic world.

In 1850, while still a student, Manet began an
affair with his 20-year-old piano teacher, Suzanne
Leenhoff, a pretty Dutch girl. Two years later, she
gave birth to Manet's son. To reveal this was
unthinkable, given Manet's background and
character; besides, his father would never give his
blessing to such a 'bad' marriage. So with his
mother's help, Manet set up Suzanne in lodgings.
In years to come, even after they married, Suzanne
was to pass off their child, Léon-Edouard Koëlla,
as her brother, and Manet always kept up the
official pretence of being Léon's godfather.

Manet studied under Couture for six years, a
period broken only by a visit to Italy in 1853, where

he copied the Old Masters in Venice, Florence and Rome. Then in 1856, he left Couture and began to work on his own. But before settling down, he travelled to Holland, Germany, Austria and again to Italy, visiting galleries and making sketches.

Manet worked hard, but still found time for pleasure, and above all the evening parties and café discussions where he met the cream of artistic society. With his ease of manner and irresistible charm, Manet always attracted friends, including the brilliant poet Charles Baudelaire whom he met in 1858. The two were to remain loyal companions until Baudelaire's death from syphilis, nine years later. Manet was a generous friend, often lending Baudelaire money, just as he helped Claude Monet financially.

DISAPPOINTMENT AND SCANDAL

In 1859 Manet submitted his first canvas to the Salon – *The Absinthe Drinker* (p.18). He expected success, but the painting was rejected almost unanimously. Bitterly disappointed, but still courting official favour, Manet set to work on the *Concert in the Tuileries Gardens* (p.12), which shows a fashionable Paris crowd, in all the finery of their contemporary dress, sitting out under the trees. Because of its lukewarm reception among his friends, Manet decided not to submit the picture to the 1862 Salon. But the two paintings he did submit were both accepted – and this in spite of a severe jury. Manet's confidence increased and at last he felt he had proved himself to his parents. The success was fortunately timed, for his father died later that year.

At a private exhibition early in 1863, Manet was shocked and wounded by the hostile reception to his *Concert in the Tuileries Gardens*. Nevertheless, he

The Salon des Refusés

Every year thousands of paintings were rejected by the jury for exhibition at the Salon. In 1863, over half of the 5,000 paintings submitted were thrown out. The artists complained so loudly and bitterly that the Emperor, Napoleon III, decided to take notice. On 24 April the official newspaper carried the announcement that a special exhibition would be held of the rejected pictures – the notorious Salon des Refusés. At last the public could make up its own mind whether the jury had been correct or the artists' complaints were justified.

Jean-Loup Charmet

Rejected masterpieces
Among the stacks of canvases rejected from the 1863 Salon was Manet's Luncheon on the Grass *(p.24). The pictures were kept in the Palais d'Industrie, each marked with an 'R' (for Refusé) on the back.*

Leader of a 'school'
(right) During the 1860s Manet was hailed as the leader of a new, anti-Establishment school, and later as the 'Father of Impressionism'. Henri Fantin-Latour's painting Studio in the Batignolles Quarter (1870) *shows him surrounded by his 'disciples'. Monet, peering out of the right-hand corner, and Renoir, his head framed by the picture on the wall, are among them.*

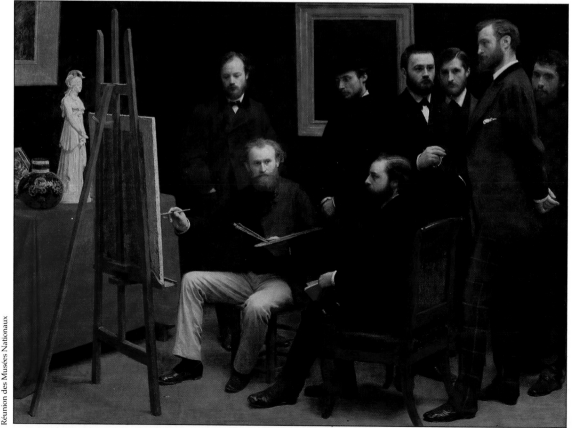

Réunion des Musées Nationaux

Musée d'Orsay, Paris

Napoleon III
*When Napoleon III authorized the Salon des Refusés,
he no doubt wanted to demonstrate that the Salon
jury had been justified in its selections. He himself was
not a good judge of painting.*

Manet/Battle of the Kearsarge and the Alabama (1864)/Private Collection

An eye-witness report
*In 1864, at the height of the American Civil War, a
battle between two American ships took place just outside
Cherbourg. Manet witnessed and painted the encounter.*

decided to submit a new painting, *The Luncheon on
the Grass* (p.24), to the Salon of 1863. The picture
was rejected, then exhibited instead at the newly
established Salon des Refusés.

Here, the works that had been excluded from
the Salon could all be hung – and Manet found
himself in the distinguished company of artists like
Cézanne and Whistler. The Salon des Refusés
drew enormous crowds. They came mainly to
ridicule, but Manet's contribution provoked
outright fury. The public, from whom Manet in his
ingenuous way had expected approval, jeered and
scoffed at the 'indecency' of a nude woman sitting
casually on the grass with clothed men – clothed
moreover, in modern suits!

In spite of himself, and his desire to be
recognized officially, Manet was soon acquiring a
reputation as the leader of a school of non-
conformist artists. And when in 1865 the Salon
accepted and exhibited the nude *Olympia* (p.26),
an even greater storm broke out. Critics and public
alike were scandalized by what they saw. Here
was a naked prostitute – a 'female gorilla' – gazing
candidly and unashamedly from the picture,
masquerading as a classical Venus. Morals were

outraged; surely the artist had deliberately chosen
to sneer at tradition. Manet was thrown into a deep
depression by the extraordinary violence of the
public's reaction and for a time was unable to
paint. He took himself off to Spain for a break, and
was bowled over by the paintings of Velázquez.

MAN-ABOUT-TOWN

Although these were years of struggle in terms
of his work, Manet had the comfort of no longer
being in need of money. His father's death had left
him comfortably off – and free to marry Suzanne.
Together, he and Suzanne led a busy social life,
entertaining and holding musical evenings. In
addition, Manet still frequented the fashionable
cafés, in particular the Café Guerbois, where every
Thursday tables were set aside for Manet's 'court',
which included Whistler, the photographer
Nadar, Renoir, Degas and Monet. Here he met the
novelist Emile Zola, who became a champion of
Manet's art.

Now 35, Manet was far from making a living
from his paintings. Still hoping to convert the
public, he mounted an expensive private

Manet/Country House at Rueil (1882)/National Gallery of Victoria, Melbourne

art dealer Paul Durand-Ruel bought some 30 canvases from Manet and when, in addition, his canvases were accepted by the Salon for two years running, success seemed assured.

Manet was now 40. Under the influence of the younger painters he mingled with, he had begun experimenting with open-air painting and his palette was becoming lighter. At Argenteuil, he painted side by side with Monet and Renoir in a brighter, more spontaneous style. However, he still felt the right approach was through the official channel of the Salon, and so he refused to take part in the 1874 exhibition mounted by the group of Impressionists. Yet Manet was sympathetic to their aims and a loyal defender of their work.

A TERRIBLE ILLNESS

Throughout the 1870s, Manet's fortunes at the Salon continued to be uneven. With the critics, however, his work was slowly gaining ground and his technique was more virtuoso than ever before. But in the late 1870s, Manet became aware for the first time of his ill-health. His left foot was hurting and he experienced bouts of extreme tiredness and lightning pains throughout his body. For a while he was content to believe it was rheumatism and nervous exhaustion. But soon it was diagnosed as *locomotor ataxia*, a disease sometimes associated with the later stages of syphilis.

Manet took a course of treatment at Bellevue, just outside Paris. He continued painting, although he increasingly used pastels, which he found less physically taxing than oils. In 1880 he rented a villa near the Park of Versailles where he went to convalesce. A true city man, Manet was never very happy when not in Paris and with his symptoms temporarily relieved, he flung himself once more into his work and his social life.

exhibition at the Paris World Fair of 1867. The result was depressingly predictable: people came in droves to see Manet's work, but to mock rather than to admire. He had unexpected success at the Salons of 1868 and 1869, but the critics and public maintained their hostility. Manet's nerves were so strained by the years of criticism that he even challenged a journalist acquaintance, Edmond Duranty, to a duel on account of an adverse newspaper article. Fortunately, the fight was quickly stopped and Manet offered his opponent his boots, as a token of friendship.

In July 1870, Manet's work was interrupted by the outbreak of the Franco-Prussian War. Serving as a lieutenant in the National Guard, he remained in Paris for the duration of the fighting, while sending his family to Oloron in the Pyrenees. After months of some hardship in besieged Paris, Manet joined his mother, wife and 'godson' early in 1871. By May they were back in Paris, where they lived through the end of the Commune. As the events of the past year took their toll, Manet had a nervous collapse and was sent to Boulogne to recover.

But that same year, his fortunes changed. The

The last summer
(above) In the summer of 1882, Manet rented a charming villa at Rueil, outside Paris. By this time he was desperately ill, crippled by a terrible disease of the nervous system. Just before he returned to Paris, he drew up his will.

Unrequited love
In his last years, Manet conceived a passion for a young woman called Isabelle Lemonnier. He painted her, sketched her and sent her letters and poems: 'I would kiss you, had I the courage', he wrote. Isabelle, however, was unimpressed by her middle-aged admirer.

Manet/Woman in a Large Hat/Sterling and Francine Clark Art Institute, Mass.

A late honour
(left) Throughout his career Manet craved official recognition, but it was only in 1881 that he was awarded the coveted Légion d'Honneur. And this was largely through his friend, Antonin Proust – the newly-appointed Arts Minister – pulling strings. For Manet, however, it had come 'too late to repair 20 years' lack of success'.

Manet's tomb
(above) On 20 April 1883 Manet had his leg amputated and soon afterwards fell into a fever. He died 10 days later and was buried in the Passy Cemetery in Paris.

Manet's work now seemed much less revolutionary than in the 1860s, and in 1881 he was awarded a second-class medal by the Salon. At the end of this year, he was even named a Chevalier of the Légion d'Honneur, largely through the efforts of his lifelong friend Antonin Proust, the Minister of Arts. But for Manet, acceptance had come too late to be properly enjoyed. Crippled by pain and increasingly irritable, he underwent further medical treatment, but his condition deteriorated. He spent the summer of 1882 in the country, where he drew up his will, and returned to Paris a dying man.

In March 1883, gangrene set in and Manet's left leg was amputated on 20 April. On 30 April he died, in terrible pain, aged 51. 'An appalling death!' lamented his sister-in-law Berthe Morisot 'Death in one of its most horrible aspects.' The next day, the 1883 Salon opened its doors to the public.

Lessons with Berthe Morisot

In 1868 Manet was introduced to Berthe Morisot and her sister during a copying session at the Louvre. 'The demoiselles Morisot are charming', he wrote afterwards. 'Too bad they are not men.' Berthe was a very talented painter, who had studied under the influential artist, Camille Corot. She was a great admirer of Manet's work and eagerly sought his friendship and advice. Manet also learned some valuable lessons from her: it was Berthe, it seems, who persuaded him to paint in the open air. A beautiful young woman, she often posed for Manet, appearing in masterpieces like *The Balcony* (p.31). However, after her marriage to Manet's brother Eugène in 1874, she never sat for him again, although they remained good friends.

A striking subject
(left) From their first meeting, Manet was captivated by Berthe Morisot's ravishing good-looks. This portrait of Berthe Morisot with a Bunch of Violets *(1872) was painted when she was 31 years old.*

An intimate art
As an artist, Berthe Morisot specialized in gentle domestic scenes painted in a delicate Impressionist style.

Private Collection

Berthe Morisot/Pasie Sewing in the Garden (1881)/Musée des Beaux-Arts, Pau

A Painter of Modern Life

An elegant man-about-town, Manet was above all the painter of contemporary Parisian life. He took his subjects from low life as well as high society, and was never really happy away from the capital.

Of all the great artists of the 19th century, Manet is perhaps the hardest to categorize. He was seen as a revolutionary, but he craved conventional academic success and honours; he was part of the circle of the Impressionists, but he never exhibited with them; he was above all a painter of modern life, but his reverence for the Old Masters was profounder than that of almost any of his contemporaries. Some critics have accused him of lack of imagination, saying that he could paint only what he saw in front of him, while for others his paintings are among the most complex and subtle of his age.

These contradictions reflect the enormous variety of Manet's art and his undogmatic approach to everything connected with it. He painted landscapes, everyday scenes, still-lifes, portraits, traditional religious subjects, incidents from modern history and some subjects, such as

The Cats' Rendezvous (1868)
(below) Manet was a brilliant printmaker, excelling at both etching and lithography. This lithograph was used as a poster to advertise a book on cats by Manet's friend Champfleury (both men were cat-lovers). Many contemporaries found the sexual explicitness of the poster shocking.

Ny Carlsberg Glyptotek, Copenhagen

The Absinthe Drinker (1859)
(above) One of Manet's most ambitious early works, this was rejected by the Salon jury and criticized for its uncompromising naturalism – subjects from the seamy side of life were considered suitable only if they were comic or picturesque. Manet's model was a drunken rag and bone man.

Museum of Fine Arts, Boston

Musée d'Orsay, Paris

Pinks and Clematis (1882)
(above) The last pictures Manet produced were flower paintings. This exquisitely simple group was one of a series of flower paintings he did in the last year of his life, when his crippling illness forced him to confine himself to working on a small scale.

The Dead Toreador (1864)
(below) In 1864 Manet exhibited a Bull-Fighting Episode, *which was severely criticized. Manet himself was not happy with the composition, so he cut it up to make two separate paintings (of which this is one) and destroyed the parts left over.*

National Gallery of Art, Washington

The Luncheon on the Grass (p.24), that defy all categorization. Unlike most of his contemporaries, he rarely repeated favourite themes.

His paintings range from intimate sketches to ambitious large-scale canvases meant to impress on the walls of the Salon, and he was also a superb draughtsman and pastellist, as well as a masterful printmaker. In all these fields he showed an intuitive feeling for the characteristics of his materials, and like many great artists he was reluctant to theorize: he was once prompted to publish his views on art, but he replied 'No, I would put it badly, since it is not my business and everyone ought to stick to his own trade.'

SPONTANEOUS SKETCHES

Although Manet's work is so varied, it was based largely on his skill in drawing – in capturing spontaneously the life he saw around him in the boulevards and cafés of Paris. He carried notebooks with him everywhere, sketching constantly. A contemporary described his tireless observation: 'The least object or detail of an object that caught his attention was immediately fixed on paper. These sketches, these brief drawings that one might call instantaneous, show with what certainty he seized on the characteristic trait and the decisive moment.'

The sense of spontaneity that Manet captured

Young Woman with Blue Eyes (1878)
Manet loved painting beautiful young women and he found pastel the perfect medium to capture the softness of their skin. Here Manet's touch is so delicate that the colour seems almost to have been breathed on to the paper.

Musée d'Orsay, Paris

TRADEMARKS

The Beauty of Black

The Impressionists banished black from their palettes, endeavouring to make their paintings bright and full of light. Manet, however, saw black as a positive, not a negative force in his painting and used it so skilfully in contrast with lighter tones that it takes on a sparkle of its own.

Unlike most of the Impressionists, Manet was a skilful printmaker, so he was used to thinking in terms of bold contrasts of black of white.

in his drawings was crucial to his art, and his working method was geared to retaining it. His friendship with the Impressionists led him to enjoy painting out-of-doors, but it was not so easy to keep a feeling of freshness when he was in the studio, where most of his work was done.

FAMILY MODELS

Manet overcame the conventionality and the formality that could come from working with professional models by relying mainly on his family and friends to pose for him. His brothers and brothers-in-law, his sister-in-law Berthe Morisot, and various painter and critic friends appear regularly in his paintings. But Manet had no fixed rules: for his two most famous works, *The Luncheon on the Grass* and *Olympia* (p.26), he employed the same professional model, Victorine Meurent. Both these paintings were carefully planned, but more often, as his friend Emile Zola remarked, 'In beginning a picture, he could never say how it would come out.'

Manet's paintings do indeed often look anything but planned, as if everything had come right for him in the heat of inspiration. Often,

however, he endured a long struggle to get the effects he wanted. He was ruthlessly self-critical and would repaint passages again and again, or even destroy the canvas and start afresh, until he was satisfied. The novelist George Moore had his portrait painted by Manet (the picture has unfortunately been destroyed), and described the exhilarating way in which the artist worked: 'I saw him scrape off the rough paint and prepare to start afresh. Half an hour after he had entirely repainted the hair; every time it came out brighter and fresher and the painting never seemed to lose anything in quality.'

Although his subject matter was usually firmly of the present, Manet often looked to the art of the past for inspiration. He made numerous copies of the Old Masters, studying assiduously in the Louvre, and also on his journeys to Holland, Italy and Spain. In Spain he was overwhelmed by the work of Velázquez, and Manet's liking for clean, bold forms against plain backgrounds, as in *The Fifer* (p.28), reflects the influence of the great 17th century master.

Manet was also influenced by Japanese prints – their strong colours and flat patterning appealed greatly to him. In his *Portrait of Emile Zola* (p.30),

he included a Japanese print on the wall behind the sitter, together with an engraving after a painting by Velázquez and a print of his own *Olympia*, the whole forming a kind of artistic manifesto.

The distinctive boldness of Manet's work depends not only on his composition and colouring, but also on his handling of paint, particularly the way he treated light and shade. The normal academic practice was to produce very fine gradations, so that dark blended imperceptibly into light, but Manet liked stark contrasts of light and shadow. The effect that this produces in his paintings is similar to that seen in photographs taken by flash, where forms seem clear but rather flattened. This lack of traditional modelling enraged contemporary critics, one of whom wrote of *Olympia*: 'The shadows are indicated by more or less large smears of blacking . . . The least beautiful woman has bones, muscles, skin, and some sort of colour. Here there is nothing.'

A FOUNDER OF MODERN ART

Manet no longer enrages the critics, but he continues to perplex. Although he is universally recognized as one of the giants of 19th-century art and his luscious brushwork is one of its chief glories, there is still much about his work that resists explanation. Often, as in his last great masterpiece, *A Bar at the Folies-Bergère* (p.33), his characterization is enigmatic or non-committal; indeed his paintings often seem to be about painting rather than about the ostensible subject. In this concern with purely visual phenomena, free of all literary, anecdotal or moralistic connections, he stands as one of the founding figures of modern art.

Boating (1874)
This delightful painting is one of the boldest of Manet's open-air scenes, done at a time when he was in close contact with Monet and other Impressionists. The way in which the river fills the background without a horizon perhaps shows the influence of Japanese prints, but the breathtaking fluency of the brushwork (detail above) is completely Manet's own.

Metropolitan Museum of Art, New York

The Reclining Nude

Manet's *Olympia* is one of the most celebrated examples of the reclining female nude, a subject that became popular in painting in the early 16th century. At first the nude was usually shown as Venus, but soon it became fashionable to portray courtesans in this way, as in Titian's *Venus of Urbino*. The pose continued its popularity into the 20th century, when Modigliani, Italian by birth but French by adoption, became perhaps the supreme exponent.

Lauros-Giraudon

Uffizi, Florence

Titian (c.1490-1576) Venus of Urbino
(above) Titian's famous nude won its popular name because it was painted for a nobleman who became Duke of Urbino. The model may have been the Duke's mistress.

Gift of Mrs Simon Guggenheim

Scala

Amedeo Modigliani (1884-1920) Reclining Nude (c.1919)
(left) Modigliani led a dissolute life and his work often has a strong erotic charge. This wonderfully graceful and harmonious figure is often considered to be his finest nude.

28½" × 45⅞". Oil on canvas. Collection, Museum of Modern Art, New York

Olympia

After the scandal caused by his *Luncheon on the Grass* in 1863, Manet was cautious about showing another potentially inflammatory picture in public. *Olympia* was also completed in 1863, but Manet held it back for exhibition until 1865, perhaps hoping that the critical climate would have become more liberal by then. He was disappointed, and the furore was greater than ever. Although *Olympia* was part of a great tradition including works by the most revered artists, the blatant, even aggressive sexuality of Manet's model, with her direct, imperturbable gaze, made the picture seem shocking – a threat to public morals and the social order. 'Insults are pouring down on me as thick as hail', Manet wrote to his friend Baudelaire, before taking temporary refuge in Spain.

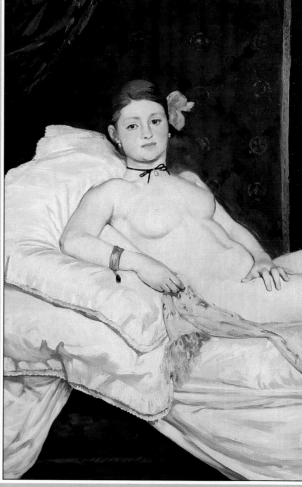

Réunion des Musées Nationaux

Flowers from an admirer
(above) The bouquet Olympia's maid brings to her is presumably a gift from one of her admirers or 'clients'. Flowers have traditionally been given as tokens of love.

Flattened forms
(right) Olympia's hand is bold in outline but rather flat; and Manet's critics objected to the lack of traditional modelling through light and shade. His direct frontal lighting gives the effect of a photograph taken by flash.

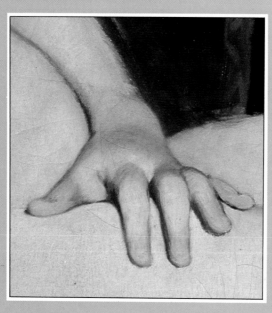

'A woman who embodies the habits of a city'
Gustave Geffroy 1892

Museum of Fine Arts, Boston

Beauty's Adornments

Olympia's eroticism is enhanced by her luxurious adornments, which are rich in symbolic meaning. The orchid in her hair was supposed to have aphrodisiac powers, and pearls were traditional attributes of Venus – the goddess of love.

Careful preparations

(above) Manet often threw himself into his work, almost in a kind of fury, but he took unusual care over the planning of Olympia. Several preparatory studies are known, including this figure, drawn in red chalk.

Inspiration from the Old Masters

Manet was humble enough never to stop learning from the great masters. He made this copy of Titian's *Venus of Urbino* when he was in Italy in 1853, and 10 years later its influence can clearly be seen in the composition of *Olympia*.

Manet's model

(left) Victorine-Louise Meurent was a professional model, aged about 30 when she posed for Olympia. Manet painted this portrait of her a year earlier in 1862. Victorine later became a painter herself and had a self-portrait accepted at the 1876 Salon, where Manet's entries were rejected. Her career was unsuccessful, however, and she ended her life as a drunkard.

Gallery

Manet was in his early thirties when he outraged Parisian society with his modern-day nudes in The Luncheon on the Grass and Olympia. The bold brushwork was almost as offensive to some eyes as the shocking subject matter. For the next two decades, until his death at 51, Manet continued to paint highly original scenes of contemporary society – the fashionable Parisian world he knew so well.

He often ventured into other fields, however, as with The Execution of Maximilian, an outraged reaction to events on the far side of the Atlantic. And Manet was also a fine portraitist, at his best when painting friends such as Emile Zola, the famous writer who defended him against critical attacks.

Illness clouded Manet's final years, but he continued to paint in spite of acute pain, and at last won the academic honours and critical respectability he had always craved. A Bar at the Folies-Bergère was acclaimed at the 1882 Salon, and with this final masterpiece Manet surpassed any of his earlier achievements in splendour of colour and richness of brushwork.

The Luncheon on the Grass *1863*
84½″ × 106¼″ Musée d'Orsay, Paris

A landmark in the history of art, this painting shocked the Paris critics. Nudes were considered acceptable only if they were suitably idealized – the more like Greek statues, the better. Manet's earthy figure, with her obviously modern companions, was too close to the real world and seemed a deliberate insult to conventional taste.

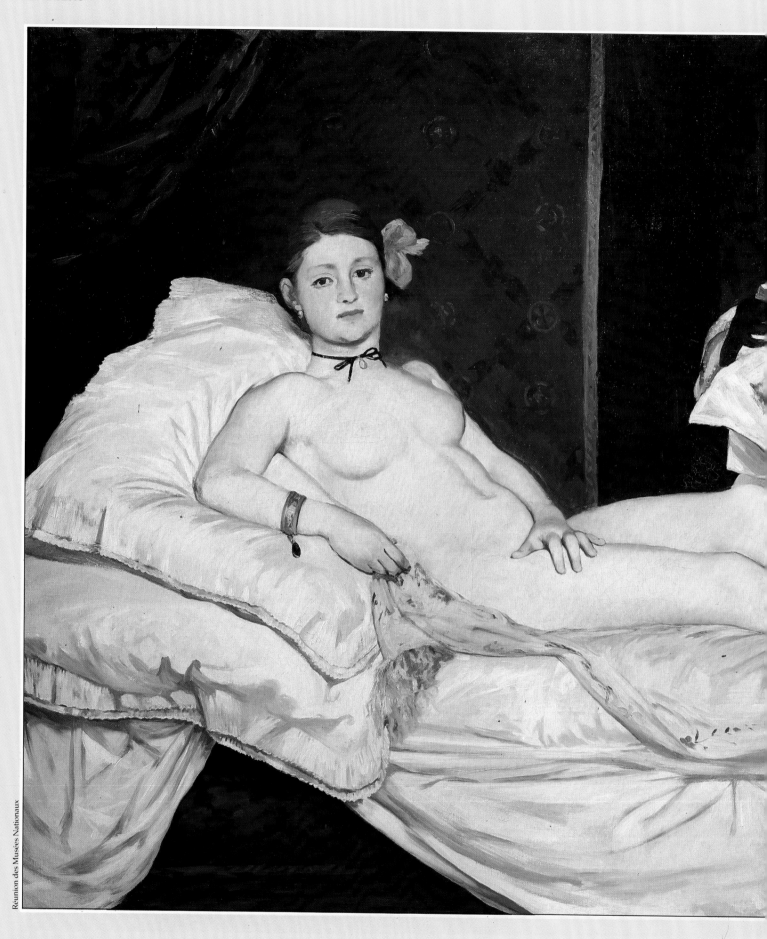

Olympia *1863*
51¼″ × 74¾″ Musée d'Orsay, Paris

Manet himself considered Olympia *to be his greatest work, but it evoked unprecedented abuse when it was first exhibited at the Salon of 1865. One critic wrote that 'Art sunk so low does not even deserve reproach.' What appalled the public was the picture's forthright sexuality: in contemporary French literature, 'Olympia' was a stock name for a prostitute, and the model's erotic adornments and challenging, impertinent gaze left no doubt as to her profession.*

Lauros-Giraudon

The Fifer *1866*
63″ × 38½″ Musée d'Orsay, Paris

A high-ranking military friend of Manet's arranged for a fifer of the Imperial Guard to be given special leave to act as the model for this painting. The boy's face, however, was probably based on Manet's son, Léon. The clarity and boldness of the figure reflect Manet's admiration for the 17th century Spanish painter Velázquez.

The Execution of Maximilian *1868*
99¼″ × 120″ Städtische Kunsthalle, Mannheim

*In 1867 the Emperor Maximilian of Mexico was deposed and
executed by republicans after Napoleon III of France had withdrawn
his support. Outraged by this betrayal, Manet used newspaper
accounts and photographs to paint four versions of the subject,
but never achieved a completely satisfying arrangement of the figures.*

Portrait of Emile Zola *1868*
57″ × 43³/₄″ Musée d'Orsay, Paris

*Zola – one of France's greatest novelists – met Manet in 1866 after he
had written in defence and praise of the artist's work. They became
firm friends, and Manet expressed his gratitude by painting this
dignified portrait. Behind the quill pen can be seen Zola's pamphlet
on Manet, the name cleverly doubling as the artist's signature.*

The Balcony *1868*
66½″ × 48½″ Musée d'Orsay, Paris

*When Manet was on holiday in Boulogne in 1868 he happened to see
a group of people on a balcony, and the sight inspired this painting.
He may also have had in mind a painting by Goya of a similar
subject. The contrast of the bold green railing with the cool white
dresses is one of Manet's most arresting pictorial inventions.*

At Père Lathuille's 1879
36½" × 44" Musée des Beaux-Arts, Tournai

'Chez le Père Lathuille' was a fashionable Paris restaurant near Manet's haunt, the Café Guerbois. The proprietor's son posed as the ardent young lover.

A Bar at the Folies-Bergère 1882
37¾" × 51" Courtauld Institute Galleries, London

A barmaid called Suzon was the model for Manet's last great masterpiece, set in the famous Paris night-club. Manet worked slowly on the painting, incapacitated by the illness that was soon to kill him.

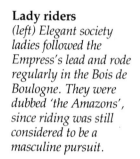

Fashionable Paris

Both as an artist and a gentleman of leisure, Manet delighted in the fashionable life of Paris. He frequented the smartest cafés on the boulevards, and enjoyed the social functions of high society.

For the well-to-do Parisian, life in the second half of the 19th century provided abundant pleasures. The French court set the style, with extravagant fashions, modish leisure pursuits, glittering balls and receptions. But the industrial age had also created an affluent middle class, as keen as the upper classes to parade its prosperity.

The social day began at noon for the fashionable 'boulevardiers' of the city. The wide pavements would be crowded with strollers like Manet, who might stop for a drink or for lunch at one of the fashionable cafés – Tortoni's, for instance, or the Café Riche, which was open from 11 am until well after midnight. The Café Riche attracted 'men-about-town, actors and artists, all the Parisians who live with elegance, comfort and money,' according to a contemporary. The composer Jacques Offenbach was a regular customer, along with Baudelaire and Manet.

OPEN-AIR CONCERTS

During the afternoon, the fashionable upper middle classes might stroll in the garden of the Tuileries, or attend one of the regular open-air music concerts staged there. Situated right in the heart of the city, the palace of the Tuileries had been the Paris home of the French monarchs for three centuries. It offered beautifully landscaped grounds, and avenues bordered by orange trees, terraces and classical statues.

Another favourite haunt of Parisian society was the Bois de Boulogne, transformed in the 1850s from a near wilderness to a landscaped park in the style of London's Hyde Park. For the fashionable lady, a carriage drive in the Bois de Boulogne each afternoon was a social necessity. In the summer, gondolas took visitors across to an island on the lake; in winter, there was ice-skating and sledging, the latter a favourite pastime for the well-to-do, in spite of its lack of sophistication.

The Bois de Boulogne
(right) The Bois de Boulogne, newly landscaped with a splendid lake, quickly became popular with the Parisian leisured classes, who toured the park in open carriages.

Fogg Art Museum, Harvard University, Massachusetts

Lady riders
(left) Elegant society ladies followed the Empress's lead and rode regularly in the Bois de Boulogne. They were dubbed 'the Amazons', since riding was still considered to be a masculine pursuit.

Bulloz

Days at the races

(left) The thrill of horse-racing and the bright social spectacle attracted many well-to-do Parisians, including Manet. During the 1860s he made frequent visits with his friend Edgar Degas to the new racecourse at Longchamp, on the outskirts of the city.

Tortoni's restaurant

(below) At Tortoni's, on the Boulevard des Italiens, elegantly dressed gentlemen would sit on the terrace or – in the evening – gather in the salon of the restaurant. Manet and his friends met here regularly during the 1860s – a table was reserved on Friday evenings.

Musée Carnavalet, Paris

Musée Carnavalet, Paris

During the 1860s a new craze, horse racing, swept Paris and was taken up enthusiastically by the smart set – those with leisure and money to spare. In 1857 a racecourse was opened at Longchamp, just outside Paris, and the season began each year on the first Sunday in March. Longchamp, together with the racecourse which was established in the Bois de Boulogne, gave Parisians easy access to the sport.

PARIS BY NIGHT

Evening entertainment took various forms. There were, of course, the pleasures of dining out at such prestigious restaurants as the Café Anglais, which featured regularly in newspaper gossip columns on account of its aristocratic clientèle and exquisite food. Customers dined in the café's vast cellar, which also held 200,000 bottles of wine. Private banquets were held in other suites in the restaurant, and for more intimate occasions – perhaps a meal between a well-respected man and his mistress – one of the *cabinets particuliers*, small rooms with separate staircases, would be hired.

An assignation

(right) Parisian cafés were convenient meeting places for well-to-do gentlemen and women from the demi-monde – actresses, singers and prostitutes.

Victoria and Albert Museum, London

Bulloz

Musée Carnavalet, Paris

Bulloz

On particular evenings during the season, the Tuileries gardens would be transformed with coloured lanterns and Bengal lights into a fairytale setting for grand balls and fancy-dress balls held by the Court. These reached new heights of splendour as fashions grew more and more opulent: clothes had become an important means of displaying wealth and status.

During the early 1860s crinolines had been all the rage, but under the influence of an English designer, Charles Worth, the crinoline lost favour by about 1868. Worth, who had come to Paris as a shop assistant, became the most influential designer of the century, and it was largely due to him that Paris became the mecca of the fashion world – a position it holds to this day.

Although Worth was responsible for banishing the absurdities of the crinoline, his creations were sumptuous and extreme in their own way. He made use of new and different materials such as brocade, tulle, crushed velvet and Lyons silk, and

The Winter Garden
(above) Not far from the Champs Elysées, the Winter Garden was open to everyone for dancing and concerts, and had a lively family atmosphere.

A Court banquet
(below) Under Napoleon III, the Court set the style for fashionable society throughout France. This magnificent banquet was held at the theatre in the palace of the Tuileries to celebrate the Universal Exhibition of 1867.

trimmed his dresses with garlands of artificial flowers, flounces, ruches, ribbons, lace and jewels, often hiding completely the sumptuous silk, satin or velvet of the dress itself.

COURT FASHIONS

Extravagant fashions on this scale demanded great wealth – and as a result, Court invitations were not always joyfully received. One lady guest at a Court ball in the 1860s was reported as saying that she had been invited to a house-party held by the Court and 'had to sell a flour mill to meet the expense'. This is perhaps less surprising in the context – for a few days' stay, it was considered necessary to take about twenty dresses, eight day costumes, seven ball dresses, five gowns for tea and a hunting outfit.

Bulloz

As women's fashions became increasingly fussy, men's clothing underwent a revolution in favour of sobriety. Towards the middle of the century, black or dark suits began to be worn by men of all ranks, until they became almost an obligatory everyday uniform.

Originally copied from the clothes worn by English country gentlemen, the dark, sober tail coat became a hallmark of respectability that, on the surface at least, gave the appearance of equality between different ranks. The less wealthy were helped considerably by the boom in ready-made suits, but men of wealth would still have their clothes made for them.

Decoration, strong colours and luxurious materials disappeared almost entirely from the male wardrobe as neckcloths or cravats became the only permissible outlet for individuality or frivolity. The overall effect was grave, even sombre, as can be seen in Manet's *The Concert at the Tuileries*, in which – almost without exception – the men are dressed in black frock coats and top hats.

Hats were important for both sexes; indeed, it was considered almost indecent to appear in public without one. The 1860s man-about-town favoured top hats: the taller these were, the more elegant the wearer. For women, simple bonnets were fast being replaced by hats richly decorated with feathers, flowers and artificial fruit.

LAVISH SPECTACLE

At the theatre and opera, extravagance and flamboyance were again the order of the day. Lavish spectacle was highly prized: one production of Cinderella in the 1860s demanded no less than 30 different full-scale sets. The newly built Paris Opera staged equally grand productions, with the light operas of Offenbach achieving immense popularity.

Private salons were important for cultured Parisians. At these evening gatherings, sparkling conversation was highly valued, and new artistic and literary ideas were circulated and discussed as avidly as the latest gossip.

The society of the time was essentially outward-looking, materialistic and pleasure-loving, lax in morals but with certain 'rules' that had to be followed for appearance's sake. So although it was commonplace for the well-to-do to keep mistresses or lovers (and the liaison might be universally known), publicly they could not be linked in any way without creating a scandal.

Frequently the mistresses of the affluent came from the *demi-monde*, the enticing world of actresses, singers and beautiful courtesans, known as *grandes cocottes*, immortalized in stories such as Dumas' *The Lady of the Camellias* (which later became the subject of Verdi's opera *La Traviata*) and Zola's novel *Nana*. Some of these ladies became very wealthy – and very famous – as a result of their affairs, but they were not openly admitted into respectable social circles until later in the century.

Musée Carnavalet, Paris

A ball at the Tuileries
(*above*) *The magnificent palace of the Tuileries, with its beautiful gardens, made a perfect setting for grand Court balls. Manet moved with ease in high society and was used to the glitter and formality of such occasions.*

Musée Carnavalet, Paris

Women's fashions
(*above*) *Women's fashions grew more elaborate in the 1860s and 1870s as clothing became a symbol of status and wealth amongst the middle and upper-middle classes.*

The Paris Opera
(*left*) *The sumptuous auditorium of the Paris Opera – completed in 1875 – made an extravagant setting for fancy dress balls, which were popular amusements amongst fashionable Paris society.*

Musée Carnavalet/Lauros-Giraudon

A Year in 1867
the Life

Europe watched nervously as Napoleon III, Emperor of France, embarked on new adventures to increase his country's power. In the event, his fortunes seesawed wildly, with a disaster in Mexico, a prestigious 'universal exhibition' in Paris, and a decisive victory over Garibaldi outside Rome. Fearing the worst, Britain prepared to counter French moves against Turkey.

Fiorepress, Turin

Museo Risorgimento, Turin

Garibaldi's Redshirts
(left) The Italian nationalist Giuseppe Garibaldi (1807-82) had made history in 1860 by invading Italy with an army of 1,000 men: the famous Redshirts. In 1867 he marched on Rome – then defended by France – but was crushed at the Battle of Mentana. Italy was finally liberated and united in 1871.

Royalty in France
(below) Rulers from around the world visited the Paris Universal Exhibition in 1867. At the left of this group stand the Sultan of Turkey, Tsar Alexander II of Russia and Napoleon III of France. Next come the rulers of Austria, Portugal and Prussia; behind them the Prince of Wales, Leopold II of Belgium, the Pasha of Egypt and the brother of the Emperor of Japan.

The old year drew to its close amid gloomy forebodings. 'Public law in Europe,' *The Times* declared, 'is shaken to its foundations.' Other newspapers spoke darkly of impending disaster, of 'a catastrophe the signs of which, for those who can read them, are present and can be plainly seen.'

THE DAY OF JUDGEMENT

One man who claimed to be able to read such signs was Dr John Cumming, who was convinced that 1867 would see the end of the world and the Day of Judgement. He had lectured on the subject to vast crowds in London for many years past and his predictions were treated with great respect. 'We are about to enter on the Last Woe,' he assured his readers as 1867 began,

'and to hear the reverberations of the Last Trumpet.'

The Revd Richard Shimeall of New York, one of Dr Cumming's most devoted followers, made this picture of 1867 even more dramatic and colourful. He insisted that Napoleon III, Emperor of the French, was none other than the Antichrist, the Great Beast whose reign of evil had been foretold in the Book of Revelation. Already the French Emperor was pouring his troops into Mexico, where he hoped to set up a Roman Catholic monarchy which would challenge the Protestant republic of the United States for the supremacy of the North American continent. Now, in the apocalyptic year 1867, this unholy alliance between the Roman Catholic church and the diabolic Emperor – the Great Whore and the Great Beast – would reveal itself in its true colours.

Mansell Collection

Execution of Maximilian
The Archduke Maximilian of Habsburg was shot on 19 June 1867 after a futile attempt to establish an empire in Mexico. His adventure had been supported by Napoleon III of France, and was doomed to failure when French troops were withdrawn.

Bildarchiv Preussischer Kulturbesitz

Peter Newark's Western Americana

Queensberry Rules
The age of bare-knuckle prize fighting entered its twilight in 1867 with the adoption of rules banning wrestling, dividing bouts into three-minute 'rounds', and introducing padded gloves and the 10-second knockout.

Yet Napoleon III's pronouncements at the beginning of 1867 were remarkably mild. On New Year's Day he gave a splendid reception in Paris for foreign diplomats and told them that the Universal Exhibition, which he was due to open at the beginning of April, would usher in an era of peace and prosperity for Europe. Soon afterwards an official statement announced the complete evacuation of Mexico.

TERRITORIAL AMBITIONS

Privately he had hopes of successes nearer home. He had agreed to remain neutral during Prussia's recent successful war against Austria and now he was ready to exact his price – either Belgium or Luxembourg, possibly both. He did not reveal these territorial ambitions to the Legislative Assembly, but he did make it clear that conditions for their fulfilment were excellent. Relations with England, he declared, were 'becoming daily more intimate', while Prussia was anxious 'to avoid anything which might arouse our national susceptibilities'.

In fact, things were less promising: both England and Prussia were determined to block the Emperor. 'England is bound by *every tie that can bind a nation*,' Queen Victoria wrote angrily, 'to stand by Belgium in the hour of need.' Napoleon had to back down and a conference of the Great Powers in May extended to Luxembourg the guarantees of neutrality and independence which had already been given to Belgium.

Meanwhile the Universal Exhibition had opened in a blaze of publicity and was now displaying to delighted crowds the

Royal Albert Hall
(left) The foundation stone of London's Royal Albert Hall was laid in 1867 by Queen Victoria in commemoration of her Consort, Prince Albert, who had died six years earlier. The round hall, designed by Captain Francis Fowke, is nearly a quarter mile in circumference and holds 8,000 people.

Lister's antiseptic
The English surgeon Joseph Lister (1827-1912) developed the use of a carbolic acid spray to prevent septic infection during surgery. His paper On a New Method of Treating Compound Fracture *was published in 1867.*

HOW THEY WENT TO TAKE CANADA.

The Dominion of Canada
The British North America Act of 1867 formally united the four colonies of Nova Scotia, Quebec, Ontario and New Brunswick in the Dominion of Canada. The expansion of Canada provoked tension with the United States, and the New York Herald threatened retribution.

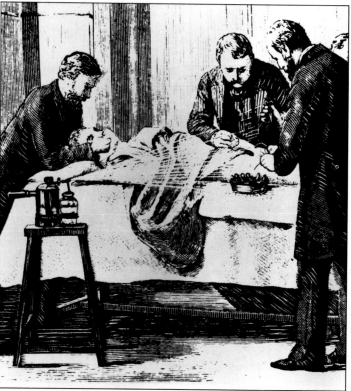

arts and manufactures of France. Manet, whose art had failed to win official recognition, opened a rival exhibition of his own in a hastily erected pavilion at the corner of a nearby boulevard. And on 6 June embarrassment was caused to Napoleon when an attempt was made to shoot the Tsar of Russia, who was in Paris for the Exhibition.

EXECUTION OF MAXIMILIAN

Another shooting a fortnight later was far more effective and infinitely more damaging to the reputation of the French Emperor. The republican forces in Mexico, who had taken over the country now that French troops had left, captured and put on trial Archduke Maximilian of Habsburg, whom Napoleon III

had tried to set up as Emperor of Mexico. They then executed him by firing squad on 19 June, together with two of the generals who had supported him.

A telegram giving the news reached Paris on 1 July, the day fixed for the closing session of the Universal Exhibition. It was taken immediately to the Emperor, who was at the Exhibition making a closing speech and presenting awards. For once his customary composure deserted him and he stumbled awkwardly through the remainder of his address, his features pale and his voice shaking. When Manet heard the news he began work at once on an enormous painting of the execution, a permanent memorial of the shame which the desertion of Maximilian had brought upon France. He was quickly informed that the authorities would not allow it to be shown.

The Blue Danube
Johann Strauss the younger (1825-99) composed his famous waltz The Blue Danube *in 1867. He had succeeded his illustrious father as leader and conductor of the Austrian court orchestra – shown below – and was succeeded in turn by his brothers Josef and Eduard.*

The Mexican disaster might have revealed France's military weakness, but it did not lessen suspicions about her intentions. On 3 July the British foreign secretary told Queen Victoria that French ambitions in the Near East must be checked and the Sultan of Turkey won over to Britain's side. A fortnight later the Sultan was in London on a state visit and significantly enough one of his engagements was to review the Volunteers, a force which had been specially formed to resist a possible French invasion. At the same time there were serious anti-popery riots in Birmingham and elsewhere.

Popular opinion, like the prophets of the end of the world, tended to see the French and the Catholics as twin evils. Some justification for this view was provided in October, when the Italian patriot leader Garibaldi marched on Rome in an attempt to wrest the city from the Pope and establish it as the capital of a united Italy. Napoleon III sent troops to defend Rome and these troops inflicted a crushing defeat on Garibaldi at the Battle of Mentana early in November.

THE PROPHETS DISCREDITED

But the Emperor defending the Pope at Mentana was rather different from the Great Beast and the Great Whore riding together to the Battle of Armageddon. The Revd Richard Shimeall contrived to keep himself in the public eye by publishing detailed astronomical proof of the exact location of Heaven; but the world's continued existence had seriously discredited the prophets of doom.

Livingstone's last journey
(right) The great Scottish missionary and explorer (1813-73) left England in 1865 on an expedition for the Royal Geographical Society to find the sources of the Nile. He reached Lake Mweru (on the border of Zaire and Zambia) in 1867 and in 1868 discovered Lake Bangweulu, where he died five years later, exhausted by his travels.

Peter Newark's Western Americana

Bildarchiv Preussischer Kulturbesitz

Mary Evans Picture Library

Marx and Engels
The founder of modern socialism, Karl Marx (1818-83) published the first volume of his massive work Das Kapital *in 1867. He is shown here with a white beard, talking to his close friend and collaborator Friedrich Engels (1820-95).*

South African diamonds
The discovery of a diamond in 1867 on the banks of the Orange River sparked off South Africa's first 'diamond rush'. By 1870 more than 10,000 prospectors were scouring the gravels of the Vaal and Orange Rivers, and the future city of Kimberley had already been founded.

Edgar Degas: self-portrait at 30/Musée d'Orsay, Paris

Degas

1834-1917

The most brilliant draughtsman of his generation, Edgar Degas abandoned his law studies at the age of 18 to take up his career as an artist. He always respected the tradition of the Old Masters, but drew his inspiration from the lively scenes of modern Paris. He is best known for his charmingly evocative pictures of the ballet dancers at the Paris Opera, rehearsing in the practise rooms, or transformed on stage.

A shy, awkward man, with a fetish for privacy, Degas was renowned for his aloof manner and sharp-tongued wit. He had only a few close friends, and apparently no love affairs, preferring to devote his life to art. In later years, as the daylight hurt his failing eyes, and he grew even more anti-social, he withdrew into his dimly-lit studio in Montmartre, where he worked obsessively. He died a lonely old man at the age of 83.

The Elegant Outsider

The haughty Degas was often seen in the streets and cafés of Paris – always smartly dressed in his top hat – but his reserved manner and acid wit kept him aloof from many of his contemporaries.

Edgar Degas was born in Paris on 19 July 1834. He was baptized Hilaire-Germain-Edgar de Gas, but adopted the less pretentious 'Degas' early in his career as an artist. His father, Auguste de Gas, was a successful banker, while his mother, Célestine Musson, came from a wealthy colonial family. Her death when Degas was 13 seems to have been the most painful event of his early years.

As the child of well-off parents, Degas received a sound classical education at the Lycée Louis-le-Grand and then went on to study law. However, by his own account he spent most of his time copying the masterpieces in the Louvre. Eventually he told his father that he could not go on with law, and Auguste de Gas agreed to let the 18-year-old Edgar take up a career as a painter. A room in the de Gas house was converted into a studio, and Edgar was set to study under two now-forgotten masters – first Félix-Joseph Barrias, and later Louis Lamothe.

Lamothe had been a pupil of Jean-Dominique Ingres, and taught Degas according to Ingres' principles, stressing the importance of drawing from memory and the Old Masters. In 1855 Degas met the master himself. He had intervened on Ingres' behalf when Edouard Valpinçon, the owner of one of Ingres' paintings, had refused to release it for an exhibition. As it happened, Valpinçon was a family friend, and young Edgar argued with him so forcefully that Valpinçon changed his mind. He also took Degas to see the 75-year-old Ingres, who gave the aspiring artist weighty advice: 'Draw lines, young man, many lines, from memory or from nature; in this way you will become a good artist.' No doubt this was what Degas wanted to hear, since his skill as a draughtsman gave him a natural preference for a painting style that employed strong outlines.

VISITS TO ITALY

During the 1850s, Degas made several trips to Italy, studying in Rome and staying with relatives in Florence and Naples. But he soon got bored with looking at the landscape, and devoted all his attention to people and works of art. During these years and on his return home, he painted some fine portraits, occasionally – as in the portrait of his Italian cousins *The Bellelli Family* (p.56) – anticipating the casual, modern look of his later work. But as disciple of Ingres, he was still committed to the orthodox doctrine of the period – that history was the proper subject-matter for any serious artist. In such works as *Young Spartans*

The young artist
(left) This self-portrait was painted about four years after Degas abandoned his law studies for painting. A sensitive, shy young man, with few close friends, he was supported by a private income and not dependent on the sale of his work.

Fashionable Paris
(right) Brought up in a wealthy family, Degas preferred to spend his time with the fashionable society of the Right Bank district, where he lived for most of his life. He had a deep dislike of the bohemian Left Bank, which he considered a hotbed of anarchy.

Sterling and Francine Clark Art Institute, Williamstown, Mass.

Bulloz

Réunion des Musées Nationaux

Musée d'Orsay, Paris

The Image Bank/Amedeo Vergani

A sympathetic father
(*above*) *A prosperous banker, Auguste de Gas was devoted to the arts and encouraged his son's artistic ambitions. Degas shows him listening to the Spanish tenor and guitarist Lorenzo Pagans.*

Portrait of a hero
(*below*) *The Neo-Classical artist Jean Dominique Ingres had a profound influence on Degas, who met his hero on several occasions, and never forgot his advice to 'draw lines, many lines'.*

An Italian connection
In the late 1850s Degas made several visits to Italy to study art. He spent much of his time in Naples, where his father was born and Degas himself owned a share of the family villa.

Exercising (p.50), he was making his own bid for fame as a painter in the 'grand style'.

At the very time when he was working in this style, Degas was also absorbing new influences, such as the art of Ingres' rival Eugène Delacroix. And while staying with his friends the Valpinçons at their estate in Normandy, he became interested in painting horses. By about 1860, he was already making pictures of horse races, going out to Longchamp racecourse to sketch the jockeys and their mounts.

FRIENDSHIP WITH MANET

In the year 1862 he met Edouard Manet, an artist who was just two years older than Degas and who came from the same upper-middle-class background. Manet was already establishing himself as an audacious painter of modern life and the hero of younger artists. His subsequent friendship with Degas involved a great deal of mutual influence, mutual respect, and an intermittent antagonism based on rivalry.

During the 1860s, Degas painted many portraits, including several of musicians who performed at his father's Monday evening entertainment. Among these were the guitarist Pagans and the bassoonist Désiré Dihau, who became a close friend and who appears in *The Opéra Orchestra* (p.57). Degas also became interested in the theatre as a subject, and embarked on his famous pictures of dancers.

He was already an obsessive worker. 'When I have not worked for a few hours', he remarked, 'I feel guilty, stupid, unworthy.' There was room in

Lauros-Giraudon

Uffizi, Florence

45

Musée des Beaux-Arts, Pau

The Cotton Exchange, New Orleans (1873)
(left) In October 1872 Degas and his brother René travelled to New Orleans – their mother's family home. Degas soon grew bored: 'One lives for cotton and from cotton', he complained. The Cotton Exchange *is a group portrait, showing Degas' uncle Michel Musson (seated in the foreground), René (reading a newspaper), and his other brother Achille (leaning against a window sill).*

his life for friends, but not for love-affairs; as far as is known, he never became seriously involved with a woman. Indeed, he once observed in a typically clipped manner that 'there is love and there is work, and we have only one heart'.

In 1870, France went to war with Prussia and suffered a disastrous defeat. Degas was called up and served his time safely in the artillery. But during the Siege of Paris in 1871, his eyesight was seriously injured in some way – Degas himself believed that exposure to cold air was to blame – and for the rest of his life he worked with increasing difficulty and had to endure the terrifying threat of total blindness.

In 1872-73, Degas spent six months in New Orleans, where his mother's family was living. Though fascinated by Mississippi life, Degas insisted that – quite apart from the fact that the bright light hurt his eyes – he could only work properly in surroundings that he knew through and through. Without such knowledge, which enabled an artist to organize and select his material, a painting was no better than a snapshot.

A FAMILY CRISIS

Degas' unwavering sense of family pride had consequences that were to affect his life deeply. In 1874 his father died and it was discovered that the family bank had accrued vast debts. Worse was to come. Degas' brother René had borrowed 40,000 francs to start his New Orleans business, and by 1876 the creditors were threatening to sue. To uphold the family name, Degas and his brother-in-law settled the debts from their own pockets, sacrificing much of their personal fortunes in the process. Degas sold his house and his art

The New Paris Opera

The new Paris Opera House, designed by Jean Louis Charles Garnier, opened in January 1875 – some 13 years after the foundation stone was laid. Degas was a frequent visitor. He had held a season ticket to the old Opera in Rue le Peletier from the age of 20, and it was there that he made his early studies of the ballet and dance classes until the building was destroyed by fire in October 1873. With the opening of the new Opera, his interest in ballet grew and the life and training of the dancers became the major subject of his work in the late 1870s.

collection, and for the first time was compelled to earn a living by selling his own art. He later complained bitterly of his need to produce something every day.

Degas' difficulties with money may have been partly self-induced, since he was such a perfectionist that he often failed to deliver commissions, and sometimes even bought back his own works in the belief that they were still in need of improvement. Stacked away, such items often lay forgotten in his studio for years; in some instances they were only brought to light again after the artist's death.

Meanwhile, Degas had emerged in an unfamiliar role, as an exhibition organizer. Together with Pissarro, Monet, Renoir and others, he formed an association to mount an exhibition independently of the official system which controlled French artistic life. Degas threw himself into the venture enthusiastically. The exhibition, held at the photographer Nadar's studio in the Boulevard de Capucines in 1874, was labelled 'Impressionist' by a hostile critic – and the name stuck, much to the annoyance of Degas.

His work, laboriously created in the studio, had little in common with the Impressionist landscapes of an artist such as Monet, who painted rapidly in the open air. To Degas, the exhibition was a 'realist Salon' in which modern subjects and the modern spirit might at last receive their due.

The abuse showered on the Impressionists left Degas unmoved. As always, he was defiantly independent and disdainful. He dismissed one critic, the extremely ugly Albert Wolff, with the remark 'How could he understand? He came to Paris by way of the trees!' This contemptuous streak impressed the Irish novelist George Moore, who spent some years in Paris as an art student. He remembered evenings passed with Degas and Manet in the later 1870s, when they frequented a café called the Nouvelle Athènes in the Place Pigalle. 'Manet', he wrote, 'sits next to Degas, that round-shouldered man in a pepper-and-salt suit . . . his eyes are small, and his words are sharp, ironical, cynical.'

A DAUNTING FIGURE

Degas had now earned a reputation as a 'bear', whom it was dangerous to approach – at his fiercest where his working life was concerned. His studio was sacrosanct, a dusty, dimly-lit place, filled with folders, boxes and equipment in an apparent disorder which no one but the artist was allowed to disturb. Few people were even allowed in except models and dealers.

But Degas could be sociable enough when his art required it. He took part in seven of the eight Impressionist exhibitions held between 1874 and 1886. He haunted the new Paris Opéra, sketching dances in rehearsal and performance, just as he later entered the worlds of milliners and laundresses. And in the late 1870s, as well as exchanging asperities with Manet at the Café Nouvelle Athènes, he became a close friend of the American painter Mary Cassatt.

Many of Degas' contemporaries believed that the two were lovers, but if so they displayed a

Metropolitan Museum of Art, New York

Degas in his 40s
(above) In this etching, the top-hatted Degas adopts an apparently haughty stance – but one which may also reflect the backache from which he suffered.

Carriage at the races
(below) Degas' lifelong friend Paul Valpinçon, his wife and baby are seen in the foreground of this Normandy racing scene.

Architectural splendour
(left and above) The elaborate façade of the Opera is topped by an elegant dome and triangular pediment. The interior is equally ornate: marble of every hue was used to decorate the magnificent foyer, dominated by an impressive staircase and lit by chandeliers.

Agence TOP/Rosine Mazin

Museum of Fine Arts, Boston

Degas' Beautiful Protégée

Mary Cassatt (1844-1926) was one of the few women painters involved in the Impressionist movement. The daughter of a Pittsburgh banker, she came to Paris in 1866 to study art and exhibited her gentle portraits at the official Salon (1872-76). It was here that she was first noticed by Degas in 1874: 'There is someone who thinks like me', he remarked. The admiration was mutual and in 1877, when he asked her to exhibit her work at the fourth Impressionist exhibition of 1879, she accepted eagerly. A warm friendship grew between the two artists, with Degas assuming the role of teacher.

Mary Cassatt
This self-portrait was painted when Mary was in her early thirties. It was at this time that she first met Degas – 10 years her senior.

Woman sewing (c.1880-82)
(right) Images of women and children are the central theme in Cassatt's work. The delicate colour and lighting of this portrait give the painting its immediate appeal, and are characteristic of all her pictures.

Courtesy of Mr & Mrs Richman Proskauer/Metropolitan Museum of Art, New York

Réunion des Musées Nationaux

Musée d'Orsay, Paris

Camerapix Hutchison/Carlos Freire

The studio in Rue Victor-Massé
(above) Degas spent most of his working life in Montmartre. In 1889 he moved to 37 Rue Victor-Massé, which was to be his studio for 23 years.

heroic discretion, leaving behind not a scrap of sentimental evidence for the benefit of posterity. Degas did, however, once make a revealing comment about Cassatt: 'I would have married her, but I could never have made love to her'.

During the 1880s, Degas' eyesight deteriorated further, despite his use of dark glasses and the attention of specialists. This was probably one of the reasons why he began to paint less, turning to more easily manageable media such as sculpture – in which touch played a controlling part – and pastel, which could be executed relatively quickly and without laborious definition of detail.

Failing eyesight was probably also responsible for his increasingly unsociable and eccentric behaviour. After the last Impressionist exhibition in 1886 he showed his work only rarely and shunned all publicity, while still complaining that he was short of money. Any reference to him in newspapers or magazines, however well-meaning and favourable, threw Degas into a rage and shut his door for good to the author. 'What a fate!' he complained, 'To be handed over to writers!'

Having withdrawn from public life, Degas relied more than ever on a small band of old, close friends to provide refuge from solitude and shadows. In Paris he had two 'homes'. On Thursday evenings he dined at the house of the librettist Ludovic Halévy, whose wife Degas had known since childhood, and he spent Fridays with an old school friend, the engineer Henri Rouart, and his family. Outside Paris, there were the Valpinçons in Normandy and others with whom he could escape from the studio, assured of

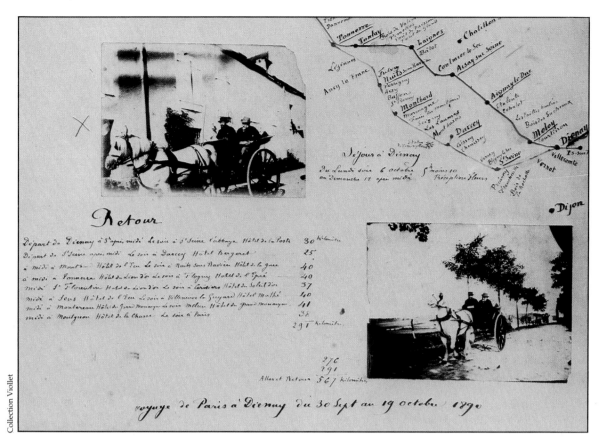

Souvenir of a journey
(left) One of the happier periods in Degas' later life was his journey through Burgundy with Paul Bartholomé in September 1890. Like schoolboys, the two artists ate huge meals at every stop, and were received by their friends with mock-civic honours.

Degas in 1915
(below) This photograph taken by Bartholomé – one of Degas' few remaining friends – shows a solitary man two years before his death in September 1917.

tolerance and sympathy for his bursts of temper and sudden depressions.

But Degas could still be good company on occasions, devising entertaining photographic tableaux which he recorded with the camera he carried about with him. And in 1890 there was one unusually sustained period of jollity in Degas' existence when he persuaded the sculptor Paul Bartholomé to embark with him on a jaunt through Burgundy in a horse and trap.

THE DREYFUS CASE

Degas' last years were gloomy, and his life was further embittered from 1897 by the Dreyfus case. In 1894 Dreyfus, a Jewish army officer, had been convicted of espionage and sent to Devil's Island; but as it became clear that an injustice had probably been committed, the reopening of the case divided the French people into two camps. Degas, right-wing and anti-Semitic, broke with Jewish and liberal-minded friends of long standing such as Pissarro and the Halévys; and the eventual exoneration of Dreyfus only served to embitter him further.

In 1912, Degas was forced to move from his studio in the Rue Victor-Massé. This – combined with failing health and eyesight – brought his art to a halt. Deprived of his only consolation, he took to wandering the streets of Paris in his long, ancient Inverness cape, at risk from the growing motorized traffic and being helped across streets by gendarmes. He survived into the Great War, dying at last on 27 September 1917.

Paris Behind the Scenes

Degas made a number of on-the-spot studies of Parisians at work. But unlike his Impressionist friends Monet and Renoir, he composed his finished works behind the closed doors of his studio.

'They call me the painter of dancers. They don't understand that the dancer has been for me a pretext for painting pretty fabrics and for rendering movement.' In this outburst against the critics, Degas sums up the intention of his paintings: their significance lies not just in the subject-matter, no matter how descriptive or provocative that might be. For when Degas painted a dancer, it was not the dance that attracted him, but the spectacle of a body in space, and the challenge of transforming it into art.

Throughout his career, Degas felt the pull of two rival forces – on the one hand the need to make art modern, just as his friends Manet and the Impressionists were doing; and on the other, his desire to respect and continue the great achievements of the Old Masters. He always saw himself as an artist in the great European tradition, whose achievements were based on disciplined drawing, composition and expressive colour.

ADVICE FROM A HERO

Drawing was one of Degas' greatest delights. During his youth he copied many pictures in the Louvre, and became a superb draughtsman. He never forgot the advice of his hero Ingres, to 'Draw lines, young man, many lines', and he realized that the discipline of drawing gave him an important link with the past that some of his contemporaries lacked. All through his career, Degas drew obsessively, whether he was scribbling down a face seen in a café or labouring for months over a carefully posed nude. Drawing was a way of sharpening his observation and of preparing for the paintings he wanted to create.

Réunion des Musées Nationaux

Photo: P.J. Gates

Lefevre Gallery

Little Dancer aged 14
This is a cast of the only sculpture that Degas ever exhibited – when first seen in 1881, it stunned artists and critics alike with its unprecedented realism. The adolescent girl with her scraggy arms was dressed in real clothes, and the original wax model even wore a wig. Degas may have been inspired by the wax-works which he had recently seen at Madame Tussauds in London.

Ballerina with a Bouquet, Curtseying (1877)
(above) Degas was fascinated by the ballerinas of the Opera, depicting them both in rehearsal, and – as here – in their moments of glory on stage.

The Young Spartans Exercising (1860)
(left) Degas was proud of this early painting of boys and girls in ancient Greece. But he soon rejected classical subjects.

National Gallery, London

In the 1870s Degas' fascination with new pictorial effects led him to investigate different techniques and media, such as pastel, distemper and print-making. Pastel suited his purpose best and became his favourite means of expression: with pastel, he could draw and colour at the same time, building up rich effects of texture and modelling without the tedious delays of traditional oil-painting. To achieve the effect he wanted, Degas would dampen his pastels with steam from a kettle, rub them with his fingers and build up crusts of colour with scribbles and hatchings.

Degas was an obsessional artist, capable of being swept off his feet by whatever novelty or discovery had caught his imagination, whether it be photography, sculpture or some new etching technique. He tried both etching and lithography, and more or less invented a new printing process called monotype, which he used to produce scores of sparkling, inventive and surprisingly intimate scenes, including witty glimpses of brothel life.

In his own time, the sexuality of Degas' art was highly controversial. Even the ruthlessly honest ballet pictures were considered distasteful by

Lefevre Gallery, London

Four Dancers (c.1902)
In this late work, created when his sight had almost failed, Degas comes close up to his figures using brilliantly coloured pastels in boldly hatched lines.

Jockeys before the Start, with Flag-pole (c.1881)
In his paintings of the Paris race tracks, Degas ignored the races themselves to concentrate on the quiet moments before the start. In this dramatic 'snapshot' composition, the flag-pole cuts right through the horse's head.

Musée d'Orsay, Paris

As a young artist, Degas concentrated on traditional subjects producing large and ambitious canvases, laboriously prepared through a series of sketches and preliminary studies. But in the 1860s, modern subjects began to exert their appeal – the bright lights and fashionable high-life, as well as more mundane scenes, of contemporary Paris. Degas turned his attention to the race-track, the concert hall and the back-street laundry.

These new subjects demanded a radical change in technique. Degas started to work on smaller canvases, sacrificing the fine detail of his earlier work in favour of bold, eye-catching effects. He began experimenting with off-centre compositions, and figures cut in half by the picture frame – as if the viewer were glimpsing an unexpected slice of Parisian life as he hurried past.

Barber Institute of Fine Arts, University of Birmingham

COMPARISONS

Women Bathing

Women bathing have always been favourite subjects for painters, but Degas' nudes seem modern by comparison with those of the Old Masters, because he paints ordinary women, stripped naked for the bath – not nymphs or goddesses posing by a stream. His intimate 'key hole' pictures did have some forerunners, such as Ingres' famous *Bather* – who seems unaware of the artist's presence as she sits waiting for her bath to fill. And Pierre Bonnard's *Nude in the Bath*, painted more than a century later, looks equally unselfconscious.

Ballet Dancers in Butterfly Costumes (c.1880)
(right and below) Degas' use of an off-centre, cut-off composition gives a suitably informal feel to this picture of two young ballet dancers waiting in the wings. Colour and incident are concentrated in one half of the image: the geometric simplicity and neutral greens of the left heighten the impact of this busy, brightly coloured right side. The detail shows clearly how Degas used layer upon scribbled layer of brightly coloured pastel to imitate the diaphanous material of the young ballerinas' dresses.

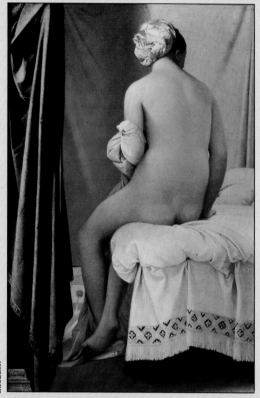

Giraudon

Jean Ingres (1780-1867) **The Valpinçon Bather**
(left) Degas knew this painting well, for it was owned by his friends the Valpinçons. The woman is seen from the back – a viewpoint which Degas often adopted – but it is not immediately obvious that she is about to take a bath. The water spout is almost hidden between her feet and the curtain.

Pierre Bonnard (1867-1947) **Nude in the Bath**
(below) Unlike the clear lines of Ingres' nude, the contours of Bonnard's bather are dissolved beneath the water. But, like Ingres, Bonnard has chosen an unusual viewpoint – high above the bathing woman.

Louvre, Paris

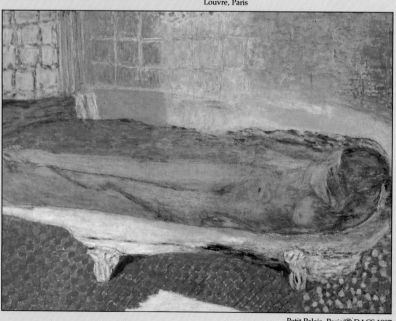

Lauros-Giraudon

Petit Palais, Paris/© DACS 1987

many of his own contemporaries. Laundresses, dancers and cabaret singers – all of whom Degas loved to paint and draw – had a reputation for loose morals, so his pictures were found shocking by both the general public and his staunchly bourgeois family. And the studies of nudes, now greatly admired and apparently innocent, caused a scandal when Degas' own suggestion that we were viewing them 'through a keyhole' was interpreted as voyeuristic.

By the middle of his career, Degas' subject-matter was clearly established: portraits of friends, nudes, dancers and singers, laundresses and jockeys provided the basis for thousands of his drawings, pastels, paintings, prints and sculptures. He was an immensely hard-working, prolific artist, who gradually retreated into the world of his own studio, relying less and less on direct observation, and working increasingly from memory and his stockpile of drawings.

Degas would very often repeat his own compositions, adding a figure or inventing a new,

Norton Simon Art Foundation, Los Angeles

quite imaginary combination of colours in his search for an image that satisfied him. Figures or horses from one painting crop up again in a different picture, years or even decades later. We are reminded of Degas' early years of study and his reverence for tradition: 'No art was ever less spontaneous than mine,' he wrote. 'What I do is the result of reflection and study of the great masters; of inspiration, spontaneity, temperament I knew nothing.'

REPEATED THEMES

Degas' tendency endlessly to repeat particular themes, such as nudes washing themselves or dancers in rehearsal, with no apparent regard for the psychological predicament of his models, has given him a reputation as a harsh, cruel observer of humanity. It is true that Degas often conceals the faces of his models, but at the same time he pays them the ultimate compliment by recording, with unflinching honesty, the weariness of their limbs and the awkward dignity of their bodies. A committed professional himself, Degas always admired professionalism in others.

Towards the end of his career, Degas became a virtual recluse, working as hard as his failing health and eyesight allowed him, still drawing, modelling in wax and retouching the pictures of his youth. He continued working even in his 70s, building up vibrant charcoal contours and blazes of pastel colours. All detail had long since gone, but he could still create extraordinarily powerful images, which stand comparison with the Old Masters he loved so much.

The Tub (1886)
The theme of women washing occupied Degas throughout the 1880s. His intention was to show 'the human animal preoccupied with herself, as if you were looking at her through a keyhole'.

TRADEMARKS

Cut-off Figures

The recent development of the camera had a dramatic effect on Degas' composition. His figures are often deliberately cut off by the edge of the picture – like a badly composed snapshot. The resulting sense of casualness belies the laboriously considered process of Degas' art.

Réunion des Musées Nationaux

Musée d'Orsay, Paris

THE MAKING OF A MASTERPIECE

The Dancing Class

In this delightful painting (see p.61), Degas captures a moment in the arduous training routine of the young ballerinas at the Paris Opéra. The viewer's impression is of an inadverent glance into the rehearsal room as most of the *corps de ballet* take a break, while the ballet-master Jules Perrot concentrates on the little dancer framed in the doorway. To achieve this sense of immediacy, Degas spent countless hours behind the stage at the old Opéra in the Rue le Peletier, studying the ballerinas at work, and building up a vast stockpile of drawings, which he later put together in his final compositions.

Every detail is lovingly observed – from the tired dancer stretching in the far corner, to the watering can used to dampen down the dusty floorboards. But the picture as it stands today is very different from Degas' original composition. X-rays have shown that Jules Perrot originally stood facing the back wall, while two of the foreground figures looked towards the spectator. One of these now has her back to us, while the other has been almost hidden by the addition of the girl sitting on the piano, scratching her back.

Giraudon

Musée d'Orsay, Paris

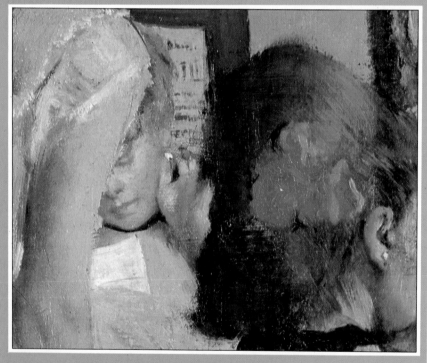

Incidental details
(above and right) Degas' details often add a touch of informal humour: between two foreground figures, we catch a glimpse of a dancer twiddling her earring, while a little dog peeps out from behind a ballerina's leg.

The Paris Opera
(right) *The setting of* The Dancing Class *is the Opera in the Rue le Peletier. Degas was a frequent visitor there from 1872 until a disastrous fire destroyed the building the following year. When the huge new Opera was opened in 1875, that in turn became the focus of his attention.*

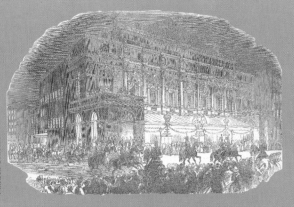

Mansell Collection

Berry/Fallon design

Collection of Henry P. McIlhenny, Philadelphia

A new perspective
(left) *When Degas added the girl on the piano, he strengthened the illusion of depth in the painting. The figures now form a funnel-like triangle that runs across the picture, enclosed by the dramatic perspective lines created by the floorboards and cornice. Accents of red run through the group, from the flower in the foreground dancer's hair, to the hat of one of the lovers by the far wall.*

A dated sketch
This thinned-oil study of Jules Perrot is dated 1875 – probably the year in which Degas altered his composition. Perrot is leaning on the long stick he used for pointing and tapping rhythm for his pupils.

> 'One must paint the same subject 10 times, 100 times'
> Edgar Degas

Fogg Art Museum, Cambridge, Mass.

Bulloz

Musée d'Orsay, Paris

Reappearing figures
(left and above) *Degas made repeated use of individual figures. This study, carefully drawn on squared paper, is the basis for the central figure in* The Dancing Class. *She appears again in* Ballet Rehearsal on Stage *(1874).*

Gallery

The masterpiece of Degas' early years is the life-sized portrait of The Bellelli Family. Painted in the tradition of the Old Masters he so admired, it achieved a new sense of immediacy, which is still more striking in The Opéra Orchestra painted 10 years later. This time the theme was modern Paris – to which he devoted the rest of his life.

The Bellelli Family *1858-60*
78³/₄″ × 98³/₈″ Musée d'Orsay, Paris

Degas began this magnificent portrait of his aunt Laura and her family when he visited them in Florence when he was in his mid-20s. Composed from a number of studies, it evokes the tension between the unhappily married couple. Laura – haughty and detached – is pregnant, but dressed in mourning for her father, whose portrait hangs behind her. Her husband sits in isolation, in his armchair.

Degas focused on a limited number of themes, and explored them obsessively. He made many brilliantly informal pictures of race meetings such as Racehorses at Longchamp. And he was fascinated by the young ballerinas of the Paris Opera, both on stage and in the rehearsal rooms, as in Two Dancers on Stage and The Dancing Class.

The less decorative side of Paris, depicted in Absinthe and Women Ironing, was also a source of inspiration for him. Such down to earth subjects were considered scandalous at the time, but no more so than Degas' nudes, like After the Bath. He returned to the 'grooming' theme in the less risqué – but equally powerful – Combing the Hair.

Réunion des Musées Nationaux

The Opéra Orchestra *c.1868-9*
22¼″ × 18⅛″ Musée d'Orsay, Paris

The bassoonist in the centre of this group is Désiré Dihau, a friend of Degas who had commissioned his own portrait from the artist. Degas chose to paint him among his fellow-musicians during a performance at the Paris Opera, and adopted a viewpoint in the stalls, close to the orchestra pit. As a result, the floodlit dancers on the stage are dramatically cut off by the top edge of the picture.

Racehorses at Longchamp *c.1873-5*
13⅜″ × 16½″ Museum of Fine Arts, Boston

In this scene at Longchamp race course just outside Paris, Degas shows the jockeys and their mounts approaching the start. Typically, he has chosen a quiet moment before the race begins, rather than the drama of galloping horses, and he is more concerned with atmosphere than with documentary detail. The colours of the jockeys' shirts and caps create a lively counterpoint against the green landscape, but they are not taken from a particular meeting – Degas has chosen them to suit his artistic purpose.

Two Dancers on Stage *1874*
24½″ × 18″ Courtauld Institute Galleries, London

*These two young dancers performing in the limelight are viewed from
above, as if seen from a box to the left of the stage. The off-centre
composition adds a delicate precariousness to the dancer balancing
on points, and the impression of sideways movement is accentuated
by the lines of the scenery tracks behind her.*

The Dancing Class *c.1873-5*
33½″ × 29½″ Musée d'Orsay, Paris

*With this informal picture of a lesson in a rehearsal room at the
Opera, Degas made a complete break from the conventional ballet
paintings of his day. Instead of depicting a famous ballerina in the
costume for her best-loved role, he turned his attention to the day-to-
day training of the anonymous young dancers in the chorus.*

Réunion des Musées Nationaux

Absinthe *1876*
36¼″ × 26¾″ Musée d'Orsay, Paris

*A working-class woman sits vacantly in front of her glass of absinthe,
while the red-eyed bohemian beside her watches passers-by. Posed by
actress Ellen Andrée and artist Marcellin Desboutin in the Café
Nouvelle Athènes, this uncompromising slice of Paris low-life was
denounced as 'loathsome' when it was exhibited in London in 1893.*

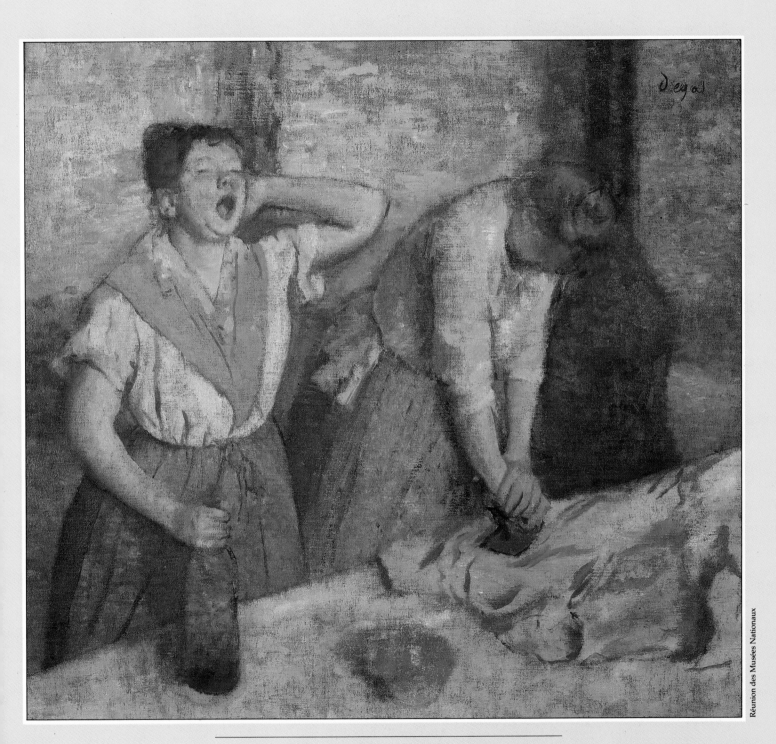

Réunion des Musées Nationaux

Women Ironing *1884*
29⁷/₈″ × 31⁷/₈″ Musée d'Orsay, Paris

*Degas made many drawings and paintings of Parisian laundresses
at their mundane tasks. In this version, one woman presses down
firmly on her flat iron, while the other yawns with exhaustion. The
bottle she holds may not contain wine, but may have served as a
mould for the starched shirt-cuffs of her fashionable customers.*

After the Bath *1888-92*
41″ × 39″ National Gallery, London

Degas returned time and again to the theme of women washing or drying themselves – it allowed him to represent nudes in natural poses, without artificial gestures. The back view he adopted in this pastel serves to emphasize its informal quality. Yet despite the modesty provided by the towel, such 'keyhole' nudes were considered obscene by many of Degas' contemporaries.

Combing the Hair *1892-5*
45″ × 57½″ National Gallery, London

*The bright colour and lack of detail in this unfinished picture are
characteristic of Degas' late work. As his eyesight worsened, his
painting became looser, yet the subtlety and acuteness of vision
somehow remain. The tension is finely balanced as the girl tips back in
her chair, clutching the roots of her long hair while it is combed
through by the maid.*

Days at the Races

A day at the races was part of the social round for well-bred Frenchmen. The attraction for many was the fashionable company, but for Degas it was the beauty of superb animals in motion.

Illustrated London News Picture Library

Bridgeman Art Library

The lure of Longchamp
(left) The racetrack at Longchamp was opened in 1857 and quickly established itself as one of the finest courses in Europe. Only a few miles from the centre of the capital, it became a leading attraction for Parisian high society.

In 1861 Degas, then 27, visited the Normandy estate of some old family friends, the Valpinçons. The estate was situated at Ménil-Hubert amid countryside that struck Degas as 'exactly like England', with 'fields enclosed by hedges, damp paths, ponds – green and umber'. The view from the terrace of the house was 'exactly like that in an English coloured sporting print'. For Degas, the visit was the beginning of a long fascination with horses and racing – the Valpinçons themselves bred horses, and nearby at Haras-du-Pin was the leading French stud of the day.

A PASTIME FOR THE RICH

Until then, Degas' own appreciation of racing was confined to the English sporting prints which were currently enjoying tremendous popularity in France. These prints, mostly of hunting or racing scenes in landscape settings, were also influential in colouring a certain view of England – of its countryside, people and customs. Racing was just one of the many English-inspired pastimes which the French adopted at this time, in a wave of Anglophilia that swept the country.

In the mid-1860s, at the time of Degas' first involvement, horse-racing in France was still a relatively recent spectator sport, and until later in the century it was principally the domain of the well-to-do leisured classes. (Manet, who like Degas was well born, was the only other member of the Impressionist circle who frequented racetracks.) Racing had existed even before the French Revolution, but it was condemned then for 'bringing confusion to fortunes and making the workers desert their workshops'. It did not spread on any scale until the 1830s, when the government began to encourage the development of breeding establishments – studs – on the grounds that faster and stronger horses would be useful in warfare.

As racing developed, France looked to England, with its well-established traditions of

James Pollard/The Start of the St Leger/Private Collection

racing: stamina was highly prized, and steeple-chasing, as the greatest test of endurance, grew increasingly popular.

The 1860s saw the beginning of a triumphant period for French racing. The highlight came in 1865, when a French horse, Gladiateur, won both the Grand Prix de Paris and the English Triple Crown, which comprised the Derby, the St Leger and the 2,000 Guineas. At this success, Paris apparently went 'quite mad with exultation; strangers are talking to one another in the street'. Within a month, a biography of the winning horse had been published and its breeder, the Comte de Lagrange, was immediately made an officer of the Legion of Honour.

Until the mid-century, France could not boast a racecourse of distinction to equal those in England, most notably Epsom in Surrey and Newmarket in Suffolk, which both had royal associations from the 17th century. But in 1857 a new racecourse was opened at Longchamp, just outside Paris, which quickly became the foremost European racecourse outside England. With its elegant stands for spectators and a wealth of facilities, Longchamp reflected the prestige of a sport which revolved almost exclusively around the smartest social sets.

THE RACING SEASON

The aristocratic French 'Jockey Club' was among the most exclusive men's clubs in Paris, open only to those with 'a fine name, a brilliant life, a taste for horses and for spending money'. The club was decorated throughout in the most English manner, with 'le Betting-room' hung with pictures of the English Derby.

The racing season began on the first Sunday in March at La Marche, a park situated about eight miles from Paris. From there, the season continued with meetings at the Bois de Vincennes during the second fortnight in March. In mid-April, a month of meetings began in the Bois de Boulogne, also in

The English tradition
Racing in England had a much longer history than in France. This view of the start of the St Leger at Doncaster in 1830 shows how highly organized the sport was, with imposing stands, massed carriages and brilliant outfits for the jockeys.

racing, as a model. The French not only borrowed the rules and organization of the sport, but also its trappings, down to similar multicoloured caps and jackets for the jockeys. Following the English example, a French Jockey Club was formed in 1833 and in 1836 the French Derby, or Prix du Jockey Club, was started, 56 years after the first English Derby was run.

During the Second Empire period (1852-70), Napoleon III was a keen promoter of racing and helped to formalize the rules governing flat-racing, trotting and steeplechasing (racing over fences). In 1866, however, he authorized separate societies to take over supervision of these branches of the sport. Gradually the French set their own stamp on

A racing background
(left) Degas' painting Sulking *shows the pervasive influence of English sporting prints. On the wall behind the couple is a framed coloured reproduction of* Steeplechase Cracks *by J.F. Herring Snr, one of the most popular of English sporting artists.*

Over the fences
(right) Racing over fences evolved from hunting, and prints of both subjects were immensely popular. J.F. Herring painted this picture of huntsmen in full flight.

Fine Art Photographic Library Ltd

Metropolitan Museum of Art, New York

John Frederick Herring/Full Cry/Private Collection

Horses in motion

(above and below) By the 19th century artists had developed a conventional way of showing running horses with all four legs outstretched – as seen below. But in the 1870s Eadweard Muybridge, a British photographer living in the US, developed a technique for taking rapid *sequences of photographs and showed the true pattern of a horse's stride. Muybridge published the results of his researches in his two-volume book* Animal Locomotion *(1887), which contained more than 700 illustrations. Degas was one of the many artists influenced by Muybridge's work.*

Henry Alken/Racing Scene/Oscar and Peter Johnson, London

the Paris area, after which there were three days of racing at Chantilly, north of the capital. Many provincial racecourses were also established, among them the world-famous track at Deauville, on the Normandy coast, which became a select and fashionable resort at the end of the century.

While French racing grew ever more exclusive, English racing during the 1850s and 1860s became highly popular among all sections of society. Although race meetings – especially at Ascot – attracted their share of high society, who would wine, dine and place bets from the privileged position of their private carriages, boxes or special enclosures, the big races were enjoyed by a wide range of people. The Derby provided an opportunity for family entertainment on a huge scale, as can be seen in William Powell Frith's painting of *Derby Day* (1858).

THE DERBY PHENOMENON

This colourful annual spectacle became a social phenomenon in a country governed by strict class. Derby Day was one occasion on which all such distinctions were blurred. But a lesser degree of social mingling was commonplace at English race meetings. Frith had apparently conceived the idea for *Derby Day* while attending a provincial race

meeting, where he witnessed a group of gypsies eating a Fortnum and Mason's pie, and a gambler attempting to commit suicide by cutting his throat.

Racing in France gradually extended its appeal down the social scale, but for Manet the fashionable side of the sport remained its main attraction. For Degas, however, the fascination was always in the relationship of horse with jockey and the movement and anatomy of fine thoroughbreds. His interest peaked in the 1860s and early 1870s, but revived again in the 1880s, stimulated partly by the photographic discoveries of Eadweard Muybridge. His famous series of pictures showed for the first time that galloping horses never adopt the rocking horse position, with all four legs extended, in which they had conventionally been portrayed. In fact, the only time a horse has all four hoofs off the ground is when its legs are closest together.

Even after he stopped visiting and painting the races, Degas kept a sympathy for the superb creatures he portrayed, as was shown by a celebrated remark he made in 1912. That year one of his paintings fetched 478,000 francs at auction and Degas who had sold it for far less was asked how he felt. He replied: 'I feel like a racehorse which has just won a race and gets fed the same bag of oats.'

Weighing-in
(below) Jockeys were weighed with their saddles before and after all 'handicap' races.

A champion jockey
(above) Fred Archer was English champion jockey for 13 consecutive years (1874-86). But his battle to keep his weight down brought ill-health and depression. He shot himself, at the age of 29.

Fine Art Photographic Library Ltd

Mary Evans Picture Library

Mary Evans Picture Library

John Frederick Herring/Gladiateur

Derby Day
W.P. Frith's celebrated panorama vividly demonstrates the social mixture that was such a feature of the greatest day in the horseracing calendar. The picture was so popular that it had to be railed off when first exhibited at the Royal Academy.

A French champion
The French horse Gladiateur achieved unprecedented fame in 1865 when it won the Grand Prix de Paris and three great races in England. This portrait is by the English artist J.F. Herring, the leading member of a family of sporting artists.

69

William Powell Frith/Derby Day/Tate Gallery, London

A Year in 1876
the Life

The year of the Second Impressionist Exhibition found France in constitutional turmoil, as the Republicans exploited divisions amongst their monarchist opponents to keep a king from the throne. In Britain, Queen Victoria was proclaimed Empress of India, and in faraway Montana another ruler had reason to celebrate – Chief Sitting Bull won his famous victory over Colonel Custer.

The Suez Canal
(left) By 1876 Britain had purchased half the shares in the Suez Canal from the Khedive of Egypt despite resentment from the French, who had organized its construction. The 100-mile canal, which took 10 years to dig, had opened amid great pomp and celebrations in November 1869.

Bulloz

Riou/Inauguration de Canal de Suez/Compiègne

The Baseball League
(right) The US National Baseball League was founded in 1876, just 30 years after the first formal set of rules had been drawn up by the New York Knickerbockers. The sport probably derives from the English game of rounders, but one US commission attributed its invention to an American soldier named Abner Doubleday.

Walter Iooss, Jr./The Image Bank

On New Year's Day France emerged from limbo. For more than five years, since the disastrous defeat and overthrow of the Second Empire, the country had been governed under a provisional constitution — a makeshift régime, whose avowed purpose was to pave the way for something more permanent. Most Frenchmen thought that the something should be a kind of monarchy, but they could not agree on its form.

The Republicans, though in a minority, had been able to exploit the divisions between their opponents. So by the time the provisional constitution was wound up, on the last day of 1875, it had been decided – by just one vote – that the framework of the new régime should be republican, with a President, a Senate and a Chamber of Deputies.

There was still nothing to stop the new authorities abdicating in favour of a king if they could agree on one. But the elections returned a republican Senate and an even more republican Chamber of Deputies. The ministry was reshuffled, right-wing monarchists being replaced by moderate republicans, and the country began to resign itself to the permanency of a republican régime.

END OF THE SIEGE

Early in April, as Degas and his friends were organizing their second Impressionist exhibition in the Rue le Peletier, the Senate and the Chamber at Versailles voted an end to the state of siege in which Paris had remained officially since 1871. It was even suggested, as a further step back to normality, that the

Sacré Coeur
(below) The famous Church of the Sacred Heart, which crowns the hill-top suburb of Montmartre, was begun in 1876. Completed in 1910, it cost 40 million francs.

Luis Castañeda/The Image Bank

Mary Evans Picture Library

Robert Koch (1843-1910)

(above) During his researches into the causes of infectious diseases, the German physician Robert Koch discovered anthrax bacillus *in 1876 – the bacterium which causes anthrax in sheep and cattle. He went on to identify the germ of tuberculosis and in 1905 was awarded the Nobel Prize for physiology and medicine.*

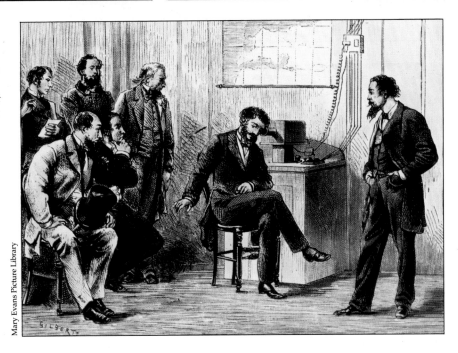

Mary Evans Picture Library

Bell's telephone
(left) In 1876 the Scots-born inventor Alexander Graham Bell (1847-1922) demonstrated a machine for transmitting sound by electricity. The apparatus – from which the telephone was developed – caused such a stir that Queen Victoria herself asked for a private demonstration.

71

legislative bodies should move from Versailles to Paris. But this was vetoed for fear of extremist riots and Bonapartist plots.

Left-wing deputies tried to get an amnesty for those who had been convicted in connection with the communist uprising of 1871. And in the Senate the veteran writer Victor Hugo made an impassioned speech asking why the crimes of the Commune should be branded, while those of the Second Empire remained unpunished. The motion for an amnesty was lost, but in June the President issued a proclamation promising no further prosecutions of the Communards.

From across the Channel the British anxiously watched developments in France. Despite the country's own royalist traditions, there was no support in Britain for the restoration of an absolute monarch, which might entail a search for glory and an aggressive foreign policy. On the whole the moderate republicanism of 1876 found favour in British eyes, especially when a man educated in England was included in the cabinet.

A CAMBRIDGE BOATMAN

'The important post of Minister of Public Instruction was placed in the hands of Monsieur Waddington,' the British press reported, 'who had been educated at Cambridge, had rowed in the first Trinity boat, and was imbued with a thorough spirit of practical reform.' With a Cambridge man to instruct them, the French could not go far wrong.

Relations between Britain and France had recently been transformed by Britain's purchase of nearly half the shares in

Samuel Plimsoll (1824-98)
(left) Known as 'The Sailor's Friend', Samuel Plimsoll promoted Britain's Merchant Shipping Act (1876), which gave the Board of Trade power to inspect all cargo ships. The Plimsoll mark on the side of ships – indicating the limit of loading – was named after him.

Mary Evans Picture Library

Tom Sawyer
(right) Samuel Langhorne Clemens (1835-1910), the American author better known as Mark Twain, published The Adventures of Tom Sawyer *in 1876, and* The Adventures of Huckleberry Finn *followed eight years later. Clemens took his name – meaning 'two fathoms deep' – from the cries of the Mississippi boatmen.*

Mary Evans Picture Library

the Suez Canal, an enterprise previously dominated by the French. The British Prime Minister, Benjamin Disraeli, had learned that the Khedive of Egypt was anxious to sell his shares and had determined to get them for Britain.

The result was what Disraeli himself described as 'a fortnight of the most unceasing labour and anxiety, with all the gamblers, capitalists and financiers of the world, organized and platooned in bands of plunderers, arrayed against us, and secret emissaries in every corner'. When the Khedive's shares were finally secured for Britain there was a certain amount of resentment in France. But the French government put a brave face on it and Ferdinand de Lesseps, the French engineer who had built the canal, publicly welcomed the purchase.

In Britain there were mutterings among those who opposed

Disraeli's expansionist and imperialist policies, but his supporters were jubilant. At a fancy-dress ball in Dublin in March 1876 one lady came dressed as the Suez Canal: 'a head-dress of Egyptian fashion; a long flowing robe of rich cloth of gold, to represent the desert, traversed by wavy bands of azure satin, embroidered with pearls, to typify the blue waves of the Mediterranean passing through the sands of the desert and bearing the wealth of the Indies'.

THE PRINCE OF BEASTS

Ten days later, on 25 March, the Suez Canal had the honour of bearing back from India not merely her wealth but the heir to her throne, the Prince of Wales, who had been on an extended

Custer's Last Stand
(below) On 25 June 1876, Colonel George Custer and 267 men of the US Cavalry attacked a Sioux Indian camp on the Little Bighorn River in Montana. The Sioux, led by Chief Sitting Bull, slaughtered the entire unit: the only survivor was a horse named 'Comanche'.

"NEW CROWNS FOR OLD ONES!"
(ALADDIN adapted.)

Empress of India
Queen Victoria was made Empress of India in May 1876, two decades after Britain's control of the sub-continent had been violently rocked by the Indian Mutiny of 1857. This Punch cartoon shows Prime Minister Benjamin Disraeli in the guise of Aladdin, offering Queen Victoria 'new crowns for old'.

Edgar S. Paxson/Custer's Last Stand/Buffalo Bill Historical Centre, Cody, Wyoming

Indian tour. Lord Lytton, the outgoing Viceroy of India who met the Prince at Suez, was astounded at his power over the animals he had brought back. 'The Prince really seems to have won the hearts not only of the Rajahs and Maharajahs,' wrote Lytton to Queen Victoria, 'but also of the wild beasts in India; for these latter walk about the deck of the ship with the most amiable expressions, wagging their tails affably and apparently disposed to fraternize with every visitor.'

EMPRESS OF INDIA

By the time the Prince arrived back in London in May, his mother had been proclaimed Empress of India. This, the most extravagant of Disraeli's imperialist gestures, was greeted with a good deal of mockery. And within a few months the mockery turned to open opposition, as the concern for the route to India threatened to drag Britain into war against Russia on behalf of the fading Turkish Empire.

The British and the French managed to maintain co-operation in Egypt itself, but in other spheres their policies began to diverge. There were a few hopeful signs – the beginning of work on a Channel tunnel, for example, and the immense popularity of a French strong man called Boulanger, who appeared at the Alexandra Palace in September and carried three men and 200 pounds of iron around the ring. But for the most part 1876 saw a worsening of relations between the country that had finally abandoned imperialist government and the country that had now taken it up.

Gerry Clyde/Michael Holford Library

Jean-Loup Charmet

Excavating Mycenae
(above) In 1876, the German archaeologist Heinrich Schliemann (1822-90) began his first excavations at the ancient Greek citadel of Mycenae and discovered some of the greatest treasures of prehistoric art. Mentioned in Homer as the capital of Agamemnon, who sent the Greek armies to besiege Troy, Mycenae reached the height of its glory in the 14th and 13th centuries BC.

Eric Crichton/Bruce Coleman Ltd

Stéphane Mallarmé (1842-98)
(above) A caricature of the French poet shows Mallarmé as the Greek god Pan – a reference to his pastoral idyll L'Après-Midi d'un Faune, *which was published in 1876. This poem later inspired the* Prélude *by the French composer Claude Debussy (1862-1918). Mallarmé is also noted for translating the poems of Edgar Allan Poe (1809-49), which had a powerful impact on the French symbolist movement.*

The grey squirrel reaches Britain
(left) The grey squirrel was introduced into Britain from North America in 1876. A larger and more aggressive creature than the British red squirrel, it gradually killed off the native species in many areas of the country.

Renoir: Monet at 35 (detail)/Musée d'Orsay, Paris

Claude Monet

1840-1926

Claude Monet was the most dedicated and single-minded of the French Impressionists. He was brought up on the Normandy coast, and the beautiful scenery there inspired him to devote his life to landscape painting. Fired with a desire to capture nature's most fleeting effects, he painted out-of-doors in all weathers. When he moved to Paris he worked with the other great artists of his circle – Renoir, Manet and Pissarro.

Today Monet is almost universally admired, but at first he was misunderstood and mocked. Estranged from his wealthy family, he endured misery and poverty in his early career, and was in his forties before his work began to sell. By the end of Monet's long life he was a wealthy man and a revered artist, but success never spoiled him. Even in his 80s he still worked tirelessly, despite his failing eyesight.

The Pioneer from Normandy

At the age of 18, Monet left a prosperous family home in Le Havre for a bohemian life in Paris. His willingness to sacrifice everything for his art had set the pattern for his career.

Claude-Oscar Monet was born in Paris on 14 November 1840, the elder son of a grocer and former sailor, Adolphe Monet. In 1845 Adolphe took over his family's flourishing grocery and ship-chandlering business in Le Havre, and it was in this busy port at the mouth of the River Seine that Claude (or Oscar, as his family called him) spent most of his happy childhood and youth.

His aunt, Sophie Lecadre, was an amateur painter and she no doubt encouraged the talent for drawing he showed as a boy. When he should have been attending to his lessons, Monet was often filling his books with caricatures, and by the time he was 15 such drawings had won him a local reputation and his first earnings as an artist.

Monet's drawings were displayed in the window of a local picture-framer's shop, and this led to the great turning point in his life. The landscape painter Eugène Boudin, a native of nearby Honfleur, also showed his work there, and when he met Monet he took the young man (16 years his junior) under his wing and encouraged him to paint alongside him. At this time most landscape paintings were produced in the studio, but Boudin, a specialist in sea and beach scenes, liked to paint in the open air, saying 'Everything that is painted directly and on the spot always has a force, a power, a vivacity of touch that is not to be found in studio work.'

Monet at first found Boudin's painting 'distasteful', but he was soon converted to his friend's way of thinking, and in the summer of

The struggling artist
At the age of 28, a year after he painted the scene on the right, Monet was still struggling to make his living as an artist. He had a young son by his mistress Camille, but remained dependent on his father, who prevented their marriage until 1870.

A prosperous background
Monet's father was a successful grocer with a seaside property at Sainte-Adresse, near Le Havre. He is seen there in The Terrace (1866), *sitting in a basket chair. Monet's mother had died 10 years earlier.*

The capital of art
(left) In 1859, when Monet moved to Paris, the city dominated the international art world – painters flocked there from all over Europe. The population at the time was about 1½ million.

Wife and son
(below) Monet's lifelong friend Auguste Renoir painted this picture of Madame Monet and her son Jean in their garden at Argenteuil in 1874. This was one of the happiest periods of Monet's life.

Renoir/Madame Monet and her Son/National Gallery of Art, Washington

1858, at the age of 17, he found that landscape painting from nature was his true vocation. 'Suddenly a veil was torn away. I had understood – I had realized what painting could be. By the single example of this painter devoted to his art with such independence, my destiny as a painter opened out to me.'

A STUDENT IN PARIS

The superb scenery of his Normandy home and the rapidly changing weather typical of coastal areas provided ideal material for Monet's new-found love. But Paris – the artistic capital not just of France but of the whole world – was a lure for all aspiring artists, and in 1859 Monet went there to pursue his studies, armed with letters of introduction from Boudin and his aunt. His father wanted him to study at the Ecole des Beaux-Arts, the official state school of art, but Monet was always strong-minded and self-confident and preferred to study at the Atelier Suisse. Named after its founder Charles Suisse, this was an independent academy where models were provided but there were no examinations and no formal tuition. Monet's father cut off his allowance because of his disobedience.

At the Atelier Suisse, Monet met Camille Pissarro, who was to become one of the central figures of the Impressionist movement, and he frequented the Brasserie des Martyrs in Montmartre, a favourite meeting place of Gustave Courbet, Edouard Manet and other avant-garde artists. Monet's growing involvement in the cultural life of Paris was halted when he was conscripted into the army, and in 1861-62 he

Key Dates

1840 born in Paris

1845 family moves to Le Havre

1858 meets Eugène Boudin who encourages him to paint in the open air

1859 moves to Paris

1863 meets Renoir, Sisley and Bazille

1867 his son Jean born to Camille Doncieux

1870 marries Camille. Visits England

1871 moves to Argenteuil

1874 first Impressionist exhibition in Paris

1879 Camille dies

1883 settles at Giverny

1892 begins *Rouen Cathedral* series. Marries Alice Hoschedé

1900 enlarges waterlily pond in his garden

1908 begins to suffer from cataracts on eye

1911 Alice dies

1914 builds studio for series of *Waterlilies*

1926 dies at Giverny

77

A floating studio
When Monet moved to Argenteuil on the Seine in 1871 he built a special floating studio so he could work on the river. This painting, made by Edouard Manet in 1874, shows Monet on the boat with his wife Camille.

Manet/Monet in his Floating Studio/Neue Pinakothek, Munich

served in Algeria. He developed anaemia and went to convalesce at home, where his family offered to buy him out of the army if he would undertake to study with an established painter.

Monet agreed, but before returning to Paris he met the Dutch painter Johan Barthold Jongkind, who was working at Le Havre and who with Boudin was to be the great mentor of Monet's early career. The novelist and critic Emile Zola wrote in 1868 of the 'astonishing breadth' and 'masterly simplifications' of Jongkind's paintings, 'rapidly brushed for fear of losing the first impression', and in 1900 Monet said that he owed to him 'the definitive education of my eye'.

FINANCIAL PROBLEMS

In 1862 Monet began to study at the Paris studio of Charles Gleyre, a successful painter of conventional portraits and figure compositions. Monet was not happy following the normal academic training of painting from the nude model, but as his fellow-student Pierre-Auguste Renoir remarked, if Gleyre was 'of no help to his pupils', he at least had the merit 'of leaving them pretty much to their own devices'. Other students included Frédéric Bazille and Alfred Sisley, who with Monet and Renoir, would evolve the Impressionist style of painting. They painted together

The Birth of Impressionism

The term Impressionism was coined in 1874 when Monet and several of his associates, including Cézanne, Degas and Renoir, held a group exhibition. A journalist called Louis Leroy made a sarcastic attack on Monet's *Impression: Sunrise* (opposite) in a review in the satirical magazine *Le Charivari*, heading his article 'Exhibition of the Impressionists'. The name stuck. Seven more group exhibitions followed, the last in 1886. Monet showed his work at five of the eight exhibitions.

Impression: Sunrise (1872)
(right) This view of the harbour at Le Havre gave Impressionism its name. 'What freedom, what ease of workmanship!' wrote the critic Louis Leroy in his mocking review.

Impressionism mocked
Critics and cartoonists found the Impressionists an easy target. Their bright colours and bold brushwork made their paintings seem crude and unfinished compared with the more traditional and sober works to which the public was accustomed.

in the Forest of Fontainebleau, and Bazille, who came from a wealthy family, helped Monet financially until his death in 1870.

Gleyre was forced to close his studio in 1864 because of an eye ailment and Monet's family, dismayed at his bohemian lifestyle, again cut off his allowance. His financial problems continued to be acute throughout the 1860s and even led to a half-hearted attempt at suicide. In 1867 his mistress Camille, of whom his family disapproved, gave birth to his son, and Monet, who was staying at Sainte-Adresse near Le Havre, was so abjectly poor that he could not even raise the money to go to Paris to see them.

In 1870 Monet married Camille, but when war broke out between France and Prussia in the same year, he left her with his son and went to England to avoid having to fight. In London, where his family joined him later, Monet studied the work of Constable and Turner and painted some views of parks and the River Thames, but the most important aspect of his stay was meeting the French picture-dealer Paul Durand-Ruel, who was the first dealer consistently to support the Impressionists. Although Monet would still know poverty after Durand-Ruel began buying his pictures, his life was no longer the tale of unremitting destitution it had been through so much of the 1860s.

In 1871 Monet returned to France via Holland and rented a house at Argenteuil, a village on the Seine a few miles from Paris. This was one of the most fruitful periods in Monet's life: he was happily married and comparatively prosperous (Camille inherited some money in 1873), and the pleasures of life on the river and along its banks provided him with an abundance of subjects. His friends often visited him, and the bridges and boats of Argenteuil appear again and again in the Impressionist paintings of Renoir and Sisley.

CAMILLE'S DEATH

It was at this period that the Impressionists were most united and in 1874 they held their first exhibition as a group. The show was a commercial failure, as was a group sale in the following year, and when debts began to mount, Monet's idyllic Argenteuil period drew to a close. In 1878 he moved to Vétheuil, still on the Seine, but farther from Paris, and in 1879 Camille died after a long illness. Monet's burden of grief and responsibility (by now he had a second son) was eased by a woman called Alice Hoschedé, the wife of a collector of Impressionist paintings, with whom Monet had begun an affair in 1876. She nursed Camille, looked after the children and assumed Monet's debts. Monet eventually married her in 1892 after she had become a widow.

In the next few years Monet moved to various places, including Dieppe, Pourville and Varengéville, all on the Normandy coast. Then in 1883 he finally settled at Giverny, about 40 miles from Paris, on the River Epte, with Madame Hoschedé, his children and her children. By this time the original Impressionist group had virtually broken up, and only Monet continued to pursue the Impressionist ideal – the acute scrutiny of nature.

Musée Marmottan, Paris

Paul Durand-Ruel
Durand-Ruel was the earliest and most important of the Impressionists' dealers. After his death in 1922, Monet told his son 'I shall never forget all that my friends and I owe to your father.'

Collection Philippe Piguet

Monet in London

Monet first went to London in 1870-71 to avoid the Franco-Prussian War, during which his friend Frédéric Bazille was killed in action. There he met the picture-dealer Paul Durand-Ruel, who had transferred his stock of pictures from Paris when the war began and would later play a key role in establishing Monet's reputation.

Monet did not return to London for almost 30 years, but he then made three visits between 1899 and 1904. On these trips he produced dozens of paintings, concentrating on certain favourite themes, notably the Houses of Parliament and the bridges over the Thames.

Topham Picture Library

Visits to Venice

Monet visited Venice in 1908 with his second wife Alice and they returned the following year. He worked hard during these visits, but is seen here with Alice in lighter mood, feeding the pigeons in St Mark's Square.

Monet now had a settled home, but his tremendous energy led him to travel widely in search of subjects, and in the 1880s he worked extensively on the Mediterranean coast as well as in Brittany and Normandy; he also visited Holland and Italy. In the same decade his reputation began to grow and his fortunes to prosper, thanks in great measure to the efforts of Durand-Ruel, who in 1883 alone organized exhibitions of Impressionist paintings in Berlin, Boston, London and Rotterdam. By 1890 Monet was secure enough financially to buy the house at Giverny he had previously rented, and in 1891 an exhibition of his paintings at Durand-Ruel's gallery in Paris sold out only three days after opening.

All the paintings at this exhibition were of haystacks, and this marked the beginning of the most original feature of Monet's later career – the production of several series of paintings in which he represented the same subject at different times of the day under different lighting conditions. Monet spent much of his time in his studio developing these series for although he still loved painting out of doors, he now realized that he

could more easily obtain the effects he wanted when he had time to reflect away from the subject.

MONET THE GARDENER

As he advanced in years, Monet continued to travel; he visited Norway in 1895 as the guest of Queen Christiana, London three times between 1899 and 1904, Madrid in 1904 and Venice in 1908 and 1909. However, his attention was focused mainly on Giverny, and particularly on one part of his home – the water garden that he had developed during the 1890s on a strip of marshland next to his house. Monet had diverted a stream through it and created an exotic world of weeping willows, bamboo and floating lilies.

He began painting the garden in about 1899, and from about 1906 it became the centre of his artistic life, for in the waterlilies, with their ever-changing patterns of colour and light, he had found an inexhaustible subject: 'my pond had become enchanted'. The first paintings of the garden were about three feet square, but they became larger as Monet's absorption increased,

The Savoy Hotel

(left) On his later visits to London, Monet stayed at the Savoy, one of the grandest hotels in the capital, from which he had a good view of the river. When the American painter John Singer Sargent visited Monet there, he found him 'surrounded by some 90 canvases'. Monet did not have time to finish the paintings in London, but shipped them back to France and completed them in his Giverny studio.

Waterloo Bridge (1903)

Waterloo Bridge was among Monet's favourite subjects in London. In 1904 he exhibited 37 views of the Thames at Durand-Ruel's gallery in Paris – 18 were of this bridge. The exhibition catalogue said the paintings were the result of 'four years of reflective observation, strenuous effort, prodigious labour'. Monet obtained the high viewpoint from a balcony (no longer in existence) at the Savoy Hotel.

Monet's final home

In 1883, Monet moved into this splendid house at Giverny, some 40 miles from Paris, where he lived until his death 43 years later. He made numerous paintings of the house and the magnificent garden he created there.

and in 1914 he had a special studio built so he could work on a huge scale. His wife had died three years earlier, but he had the love of his devoted step-daughter, Blanche Hoschedé-Monet, herself a painter, to support him, and he worked with un-flagging energy.

By this time Monet was the grand old man of French painting, and it was at the suggestion of the Prime Minister, Georges Clemenceau, one of the many distinguished visitors to Giverny, that he decided to present several of his waterlily paintings to the nation in the form of an enormous decorative scheme. Monet's sight was failing, his work on the paintings was delayed while he had a cataract operation, and he did not live to see their unveiling in the Orangerie in Paris (part of the Louvre complex) on 17 May 1927. He died aged 86, on 5 December 1926 at Giverny and was buried beside the small village church. In the last year of his life, Monet described his aim as being 'to render my impressions in front of the most fleeting effects', words he could equally have used at any stage during more than half a century of ceaseless creativity.

The Fleeting Impression

Monet painted in the open air with a speed and fervour no earlier artist had approached. But as he grew older, he saw the need to work more in his studio, to refine and perfect his paintings.

Monet is often considered the greatest and most typical of the Impressionists. This judgement reflects not only the quality of his work, but also his wholehearted dedication to the ideals of Impressionism throughout his mature life. In particular, he was committed to the Impressionist practice of painting out of doors. This in itself was not new, but Monet made it an article of faith.

None of his predecessors had worked out-of-doors to the same ambitious scale. In the early 19th century, for example, John Constable had often made sketches in oils outdoors, but only as preparatory studies for larger paintings. And Boudin and Jongkind, the two artists who had the most important influence on Monet's early work,

also worked on a fairly small scale. Monet differed from these painters both in his conviction and in his ambitions. He made outdoor painting not just a basis for further elaboration, but the central feature of his huge output.

Monet's declared aim was to catch the passing impressions of light and atmosphere, 'the most fleeting effects', as he called them, and in his dedication to this goal he took measures that often had an element of farce about them. In 1866-7 he painted one of his most famous works, *Women in the Garden*, a canvas more than eight feet high, and to enable him to paint all the picture out-of-doors, he had a trench dug so the canvas could be raised or lowered by pulleys to the required height.

Monet at work
Under a huge white parasol, Monet works on one of his waterlily paintings in the garden at Giverny. Beside him stands his step-daughter Blanche Hoschedé-Monet, ready to change the canvas on his easel.

Women in the Garden
Monet painted this eight-foot high canvas entirely out-of-doors in 1866-7. According to the painter Gustave Courbet, who visited him, Monet would not paint even the leaves in the background unless the light was just right.

Much later in his career, when he was working on a series of paintings such as his *Haystacks*, his step-daughter Blanche Hoschedé-Monet used a wheelbarrow to carry his unfinished paintings around the fields with him; when the light changed perceptibly, Monet would switch to another canvas that matched the new conditions.

BRAVING THE ELEMENTS

Bad weather did not weaken his determination to capture the effects he wanted. One observer described him working on the Normandy coast in 1885: 'With water streaming under his cape, he painted the storm amid the swirl of the salt water. He had between his knees two or three canvases, which took their place on his easel one after another, each for a few minutes at a time. On the stormy sea different light effects appeared. The painter watched for each of these effects, a slave to the comings and goings of the light, laying down his brush when the effect was gone, placing at his feet the unfinished canvas, ready to resume work upon the return of a vanished impression.'

Such accounts of Monet at work – part-heroic, part-absurd – illustrate what he and the other

Lady with a Parasol
This brisk and vigorous painting, dating from 1886, conveys the atmosphere of a blustery day – the rough brushstrokes of the sky suggest the scudding motion of the clouds. Monet had to work quickly to capture such fast-changing conditions in the weather.

Musée d'Orsay, Paris

Pictures in series
In 1891, Monet exhibited his first major series of paintings – The Haystacks. *These two, from the series of 15, illustrate his fascination with the varied colours produced by natural sunlight.*

Camille on her Deathbed
Monet's first wife died in 1879. Despite his grief, he still looked at her with the eye of a painter, noticing 'the arrangement of coloured gradations that death was imposing on her motionless face'.

Musée d'Orsay, Paris

Art Institute of Chicago

Musée d'Orsay, Paris

The Streets of Paris

Before Monet arrived in Paris in 1859, few artists had bothered to paint the city's streets. To academic painters, everyday scenes seemed dirty, drab and vulgar. But when the Impressionists began working out-of-doors in the 1860s, Paris was not just a new subject for painters, it had literally been transformed: by Baron Haussmann, civil servant and town planner to the Emperor Napoleon III.

From 1853 onwards, Haussmann had been in charge of rebuilding the capital, tearing down old shops and houses to create the wide boulevards that lead to the Arc de Triomphe and other focal points. And the Paris we see today remains very much the city we see in the paintings of Monet, Renoir and Pissarro.

Camille Pissarro (1830-1903) **The Boulevard Montmartre** *(below) Pissarro's evocative canvas, painted in 1897, shows carriages parked along this fashionable street. Rows of gas-lights recede into the distance, emphasizing the formal layout of the city.*

Pierre-Auguste Renoir (1841-1919) **Pont Neuf** *(below) Horse-drawn carriages and buses – all driving on the right – cross the wide 'new bridge' at the heart of Paris. Painting in 1872, soon after the Franco-Prussian War, Renoir shows soldiers in uniform mingling with street-vendors and ladies with their children.*

National Gallery, London

National Gallery of Art, Washington

Impressionists found was the greatest drawback to their new approach to painting: the effects in nature change so quickly that the more sensitive an artist is to them, the less time he can spend on a picture before any particular effect has gone. Referring to his haystack series in October 1890, Monet wrote: 'I really am working terribly hard, struggling with a series of different effects, but at this time of year the sun sets so quickly that I can't keep up with it.' To overcome this problem Monet began to work more and more in the studio to re-touch or revise his paintings. But publicly he liked to maintain his image as an outdoor painter.

PAINTING AT SPEED

Monet developed a free and spontaneous painting technique which enabled him to work at speed. His brushwork is remarkably flexible and varied, sometimes broad and sweeping, sometimes fragmented and sparkling. Occasionally he used the handle of the brush to scratch through the paint surface and create a more broken, textured effect. His last paintings, the great series representing the waterlilies in his garden at Giverny, were executed more slowly than his earlier works and many of them have a richly encrusted surface, the paint dragged and superimposed, layer upon shimmering layer.

Bulloz

Musée d'Orsay, Paris

TRADEMARKS
Slabs of Colour

Monet's treatment of water is both original and distinctive. He makes no attempt to show the exact forms of waves or ripples, but uses firm individual strokes – sometimes almost slabs – of colour to suggest reflections in the water.

This is a prime example of the Impressionist approach to painting. In essence Monet represents what his eye actually sees, rather than what his mind knows is there. In the hands of a master, this can produce stunningly vivid effects.

Regatta at Argenteuil (1872)

(above and right) In the reflection of boat-sails on the River Seine, Monet reveals his skill at painting water. He conveys the flickering movement of the ripples with just a few brushstrokes so bold that when enlarged (detail) they seem almost abstract. Monet's love for water – first developed during his childhood by the sea – never left him. He once said jokingly that he would like to be buried in a buoy.

Paul Cézanne, a landscape painter of equal stature, declared that Monet was 'only an eye, but, my God, what an eye!' Many of Monet's own observations seem to bear out that this was the way he thought of himself. He told a pupil that 'he wished he had been born blind and then suddenly regained his sight, so that he would have begun to paint without knowing what the objects were that he saw before him'. And he advised 'When you go out to paint, try to forget what objects you have in front of you, a tree, a field . . . Merely think, here is a little square of blue, here an oblong of pink, here a streak of yellow, and paint it just as it looks to you, the exact colour and shape, until it gives your own naïve impression of the scene.'

But no artist simply reproduces what he sees in front of him, and although Monet might strive to be objective, he was never impersonal. His increasing reliance on studio work shows that he realized that his art consisted not merely in observing and recording, but in finding a pictorial equivalent – in opaque paint on a two-dimensional surface – for the infinitely varied effects of light. And as with all great art, there is a dimension to Monet's work that ultimately evades analysis or explanation. His great series of waterlily paintings, in particular, are the product not simply of an exceptionally keen eye and an unerring hand, but also of a poetic spirit.

THE MAKING OF A MASTERPIECE

Rouen Cathedral

Monet painted his famous series of Rouen Cathedral scenes following the success of the Haystacks series, exhibited in 1891. The unusual choice of a cathedral for his subject was probably influenced by the severe rheumatism Monet had suffered since 1890. This made it arduous to work in the open air ('I endure torment in rain and snow'), so a view he could paint from a window, protected from the weather, had an advantage over outdoor subjects. The series took three years to complete. Monet spent several weeks in Rouen in 1892 and 1893, then finished the paintings in his Giverny studio during the winter of 1894-5.

Musée d'Orsay, Paris

Rouen Cathedral in Full Sunlight

(above) As the 19th century photograph makes clear, Monet radically simplified the intricate lace-like forms of the Gothic cathedral, preferring to capture the haze created by full sunlight. To achieve such luminous effects, he mixed his colours with white, rather than using them straight from the tube.

Monet's studio

(left) Monet rented a first floor room over a milliner's shop to serve as his studio. The building no longer exists, for the area around the cathedral was almost completely rebuilt after being bombed in World War II. This plan of the old layout shows how Monet's viewpoint was restricted by the narrow streets.

'Everything changes, even stone'
Claude Monet

Michael McGuinness

View from a window
His makeshift studio above a milliner's shop gave Monet an oblique view of the west front of the cathedral. He was so close to the huge building (less than 30 yards away) that the sky was almost entirely blotted out by the pinnacled façade.

Musée d'Orsay, Paris

Musée d'Orsay, Paris

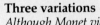
Musée d'Orsay, Paris

Three variations
Although Monet viewed the cathedral mainly from a single window, he seems also to have used photographs and engravings of the cathedral as aids to composition. The three paintings above indicate some of the different viewpoints he adopted; the one on the right is very close in angle of view to the photograph on the opposite page. Monet's lighting is subtly varied, but the cool tones seen in all the paintings reflect the time of year — he worked in Rouen mainly during the winter months of February and March.

Melting the stone
A detail from Rouen Cathedral in Full Sunlight *(opposite) shows how the richly clotted, shimmering quality of Monet's paint dissolves the solid stone into a translucent haze.*

Gallery

From the start of his long career Monet worked mostly in the open air, concentrating on scenes that he knew well. Wild Poppies was painted at Argenteuil, a pretty riverside village just outside Paris, where the artist and his family settled in 1871. Monet loved to paint the boats on the Seine with their sails reflected in the river's rippling waters – like those in The Bridge at Argenteuil.

Such tranquil, rural scenes contrast strikingly with the crowded streets of Paris shown in his paintings of the Boulevard des Capucines and the Rue Montorgueil. But the effects of light and atmosphere gradually became more important to Monet than the objects in his paintings. In the Gare St-Lazare, for example, it was the smoke – not the train – which most fascinated the artist.

In later life, when Monet moved to Giverny, he developed the unique format of pictorial series – numerous versions of the same view seen under different lighting conditions. These were designed to be exhibited as a group, and since each canvas captured a particular instant, together they recorded time passing. Poplars and Rouen Cathedral each form part of a series, but the most spectacular of all is the series devoted to Waterlilies. Monet's exotic water garden was virtually his only subject during the last 20 years of his life, inspiring some of his most hauntingly beautiful works.

Wild Poppies *1873*
19⅝" × 25⅝" Musée d'Orsay, Paris

This little painting of Monet's wife Camille and son Jean walking through a field of poppies was shown at the first Impressionist exhibition in 1874. Camille and Jean appear twice in the painting, a device which draws the eye repeatedly to the triangular hillside of bright red poppies.

Boulevard des Capucines *1873*
31½″ × 23⅝″ Atkins Museum, Kansas City, Missouri

*Monet may have worked from a photograph when painting this
wintry scene. On the right, a top-hatted figure looks down from a
window; below, a dash of pink may represent a cluster of balloons.*

The Bridge at Argenteuil *1874*
23⅝″ × 31½″ Musée d'Orsay, Paris

*Monet lived at Argenteuil, near Paris, for seven years and made
several paintings of sailing boats on the Seine. In this tranquil scene,
the impression of broken reflections on the shimmering water is
conveyed by well-defined brushstrokes of pure colour.*

Gare St-Lazare *1877*
29½″ × 39½″ Musée d'Orsay, Paris

*This railway station was the Paris terminus of the line from
Argenteuil and Monet painted it several times. He captured its
atmosphere – with clouds of steam and smoke rising from the engine,
and shadows thrown by the glass roof – rather than a precise,
detailed likeness.*

Réunion des Musées Nationaux

The Rue Montorgueil Decked with Flags *1878*
23⅝″ × 31½″ Musée des Beaux-Arts, Rouen

*This bird's-eye view of a Parisian street, decked out in celebration of a
national holiday, was painted rapidly on a balcony overlooking the
scene. The red, white and blue stripes of the French flags form vibrant
patches of colour, and in the centre of the picture a slogan in blue
reads 'Vive la France'.*

Poplars *1891*
32¼″ × 32⅛″ Metropolitan Museum of Art, New York

*A row of tall poplars lining the River Epte near Monet's home in
Giverny fascinated the artist, and he painted them many times from
his boat. In this late stage of his career Monet's Impressionist style
grew increasingly abstract and decorative.*

Rouen Cathedral in Full Sunlight *1894*
42⅛″ × 28¾″ Musée d'Orsay, Paris

Like Poplars, *this painting formed part of a series: Monet painted the
same view over and over again, under changing light conditions. The
year after this version was completed, 20 different canvases were
exhibited together, covering the whole day from dawn to dusk.*

Waterlilies *1916-1926*
78¾″ × 167¾″ St Louis Art Museum, Missouri

Monet painted the waterlily pond at the bottom of his garden hundreds of times: it became virtually his only 'model' for the last 20 years of his life. He focused increasingly on this small area, painting ever larger pictures. This 14-foot long canvas was originally the central panel of three, forming a massive 40-foot painting. The lilies themselves are not immediately recognizable – they dissolve into a magical mixture of delicate colours.

Monet's Garden

The magnificent garden at Giverny took Monet almost 20 years to create, and demanded all his artistic skills and imagination. For the rest of his life, it provided endless subjects for his paintings.

Rarely has an artist left behind such a complete record of his inspiration as did Monet at Giverny. There, in the garden on which he lavished care and attention for over 40 years, view after view conjures up his paintings: the lily pond, the footbridge, the rose trellises. The garden was really an extension of his art.

Giverny lies some 40 miles north-west of Paris, in the rolling countryside of Normandy, where two small tributaries, the Epte and the Ru, flow into the Seine. The village nestles against wooded hills, overlooking a broad panorama of fields dotted with lines of willow and poplar.

THE HOUSE AT GIVERNY

The property which Monet rented for his large household in 1883 stood at the foot of these hills – a long, pink house with shutters. Two acres of orchard sloped gently towards a narrow road, beyond which lush water meadows stretched down to the river. The garden then was formal and uninspired. A broad, tree-lined central walk led up to the house, flanked by two long flowerbeds edged with clipped box hedges. At that time, there was little to excite the eye.

Wherever he had lived before, Monet had

The flower garden
(right) Monet replaced the old orchard behind his house with lawns and geometrically laid-out flower beds. These were planted with a profusion of flowers that provided a continuous show of colour all year round. The greenhouses and studios were added later.

The central path
(below) The view from the back door of the house looked down between the two yew trees along a broad central path overgrown by trailing nasturtiums. The trellises supported roses and clematis.

Flower beds – rose trees with red blooms

Lime trees surrounded by snow drops and primulas

Flower beds – irises, jonquils, tulips

Painting studio

Greenhouses orchids and tropical ferns

Flower beds – tulips, in red, yellow, pink and rose

Russell Barnet

Dmitri Kessel Life Colorific

Roger Viollet

The Flower Garden

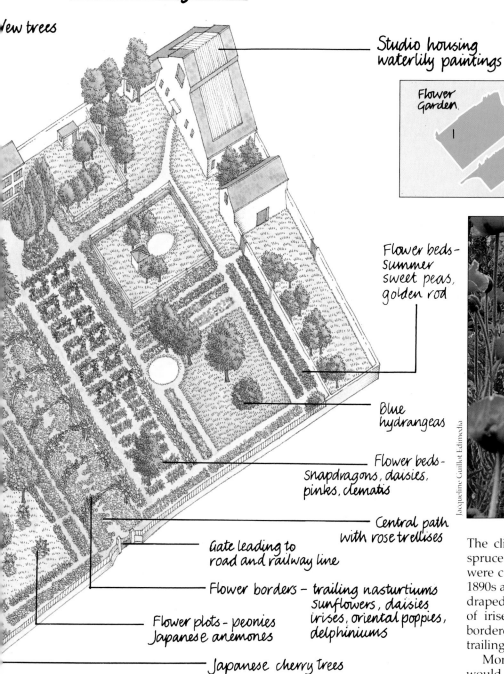

New trees

Studio housing
waterlily paintings

Flower beds -
summer
sweet peas,
golden rod

Blue
hydrangeas

Flower beds -
snapdragons, daisies,
pinks, clematis

Central path
with rose trellises

Gate leading to
road and railway line

Flower borders - trailing nasturtiums
sunflowers, daisies
irises, oriental poppies,
delphiniums

Flower plots - peonies
Japanese anemones

Japanese cherry trees

The overall scheme
*(left) Monet's garden was
in two parts: a flower
garden by the house,
and a water garden.*

Early summer
*(below) Poppies and irises
made a dazzling display of
colour, set off against dark
green foliage. Monet
preferred small blooms.*

Jacqueline Guillot Edimedia

Monet the gardener
*(left) Monet lavished care
on his garden and toured
it several times each day.
A visitor commented that:
'Monet is perhaps seen at
his best, and certainly in
his most genial mood,
when – cigar at full blast
– he strolls around his
propriété at Giverny.'*

always created gardens, but Giverny provided
scope for his most ambitious plans. It was late
spring when the family moved in. Monet
immediately reorganized the kitchen garden to
ensure a supply of vegetables, then set to work on
the house and flower garden. Trellises were
erected against the house to support clematis,
climbing roses and Virginia creeper. He chose the
same shade of green to paint the shutters, doors
and porch of the house as he would later use for
the arches and trellises in the garden and for the
Japanese bridge.

The fruit trees in the orchard were uprooted
and replaced with lawns, shaded by ornamental
cherries and japonicas and edged with a brilliant
profusion of flowering plants. New flower beds
were dug, intersected by neat gravel paths in
straight lines and rectangles, which soon
disappeared under the dense carpet of flowers.

The clipped box hedges were removed and the
spruce and cypress trees lining the central walk
were cut down – only two yews were left. By the
1890s a series of curving arches spanned the walk,
draped with climbing roses and clematis. Masses
of irises, poppies, asters, pansies and peonies
bordered the walk beneath the arches, while
trailing nasturtiums spread over the path.

Monet had approached the garden much as he
would a canvas, using the same principles that
governed his palette. Flowers with light, bright
blooms were planted in clumps of contrasting
colours, set off against green foliage – no coloured
or variegated leaves were used. Monet avoided
flowers with large blossoms, preferring festoons of
small-headed flowers clustering together to
produce a mass of colour.

FLOWERS FOR ALL SEASONS

In the early spring, yellow jasmine and Christmas
roses gave way to crocuses, narcissi, tulips,
azaleas, rhododendrons and flowering cherries,
with dense carpets of forget-me-nots. Later
peonies, poppies and banks of irises would appear
with clematis and climbing roses clambering
round trellis and arch. At the height of summer the
garden was a blaze of saffron, vermilion and blue –
aubrietia covered the ground, while geraniums,

The Japanese bridge
(below) Just inside the water garden Monet built a hog-backed wooden footbridge, based on one in a Japanese print that hung in the dining room. The bridge was draped with clusters of white and mauve wisteria.

daisies, zinnias, marigolds, lilies, pinks and cannas flowered in abundance.

Monet's garden included several hundred varieties of native and imported plants and up to the end of his life the artist took delight in adding to his collection – the rare tree peonies in the water garden, for instance, and bulbs of lilies quite unknown in France were given to him by his friends the Kurokis, who were influential Japanese art collectors.

He also encouraged his children to study botany, and in the early years at Giverny, experiments in cross-breeding made by his son Michel and step-son Jean-Pierre accidentally resulted in a new type of poppy, which they named *Papaver Moneti*.

'My garden is a slow work, pursued by love,'

Monet once said, 'and I do not deny that I am proud of it. I dug, planted, weeded myself; in the evenings the children watered.' By 1890, Monet was wealthy enough to buy the house and make still more improvements: in 1892 three greenhouses were built and stocked with exotic orchids, begonias, figs and tropical ferns. Now Monet took on a team of six gardeners who worked under his close supervision. With the head gardener, he inspected the garden every day, ordering all dead flowerheads to be removed.

THE WATER GARDEN

In 1893 Monet bought another plot of land across the road at the bottom of his garden, intending to enlarge a tiny pond already there and

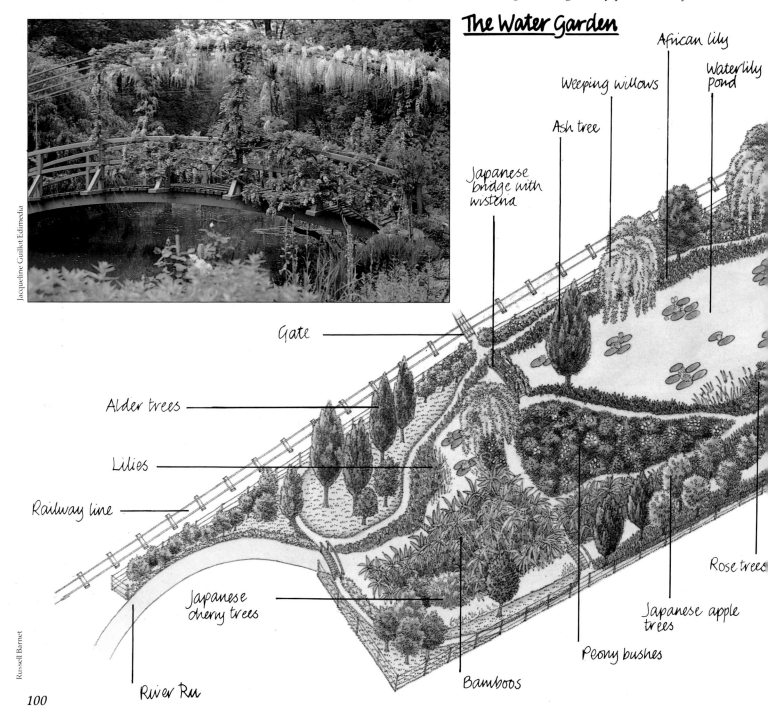

Jacqueline Guillot Edimedia

Russell Barnet

The Water Garden

African lily

Weeping willows

Waterlily pond

Ash tree

Japanese bridge with wisteria

Gate

Alder trees

Lilies

Railway line

Japanese cherry trees

River Ru

Bamboos

Peony bushes

Japanese apple trees

Rose trees

to create a water garden. To do this, it was necessary to divert the River Ru.

Monet was not liked by the villagers, and they bitterly resented his plan. Monet himself was judged to be aloof, and his family seemed to have no clear-cut social status. The villagers had already claimed compensation for alleged damage to their fields, through which the Monet family frequently trekked to where their boats were moored.

Now Monet's plans for a pond stocked with rare plants met with suspicion. The women, who washed their linen in the Ru, claimed it would be a

Poplars

Crimson rhododendrons

Irises

Waterlilies in white, yellow, rose and mauve

The water garden
(above and left) At the foot of the gently sloping flower garden, Monet created a beautiful water garden in the Japanese style. He enlarged a small pond by diverting the tiny River Ru into the garden, then filled the pool with aquatic plants and waterlilies.

supporting piers, painted in his favourite brilliant green. To this, some years later, trellises were added to support masses of wisteria.

In 1901 Monet received permission to extend the pond further, since the size and shape had become too restricting to him as he painted it more and more. By deepening the curve and extending its length, he achieved a greater sense of space, creating marvellous vistas from all round the pond. More species of lilies were introduced and soon it was the sole task of a gardener to care for the pool, for which he used a small boat permanently moored at the edge.

Just as his flower garden had gradually become a recurrent theme of his painting, so the waterlily pond and footbridge had begun to absorb Monet. As he grew older he turned almost exclusively to his garden for ideas and right up to the very end of his life he remained fascinated by the pool, with its beautiful, shimmering reflections.

Purple irises
Monet loved irises, and planted them all round the fringes of the waterlily pond; they appear in many of his later paintings. 'I perhaps owe having become a painter to flowers', he once said.

health hazard. And local peasants feared that their cows would be poisoned by drinking river water 'contaminated' by strange plants. Finally, with many conditions, permission was granted.

The mood and atmosphere of the water garden was very different from the exuberance of the flower garden. Here all was cool and tranquil. The pool was strewn with exotic varieties of waterlily – white, yellow, mauve and rose – with clumps of bamboo, weeping willows, irises and tamarisk smothering the banks. Monet added the Japanese footbridge, a simple wooden arch with no

A Year in the Life 1892

While Monet painted his serene studies of Rouen cathedral,
anarchist terrorists were throwing bombs in Paris. The French
government was in trouble – in the centenary year of the First
Republic, even the clergy showed their scorn, by preaching anti-
republican sermons. And some of the country's most famous names
were brought to grief in the financial scandal over the Panama Canal.

On New Year's Day at Cannes, on the newly fashionable French Riviera coast, the novelist Guy de Maupassant made a dramatic attempt to commit suicide. He first held a revolver to his head and pulled the trigger six times, only to find the chambers empty; then he seized a razor and slashed his throat, but was disarmed before he hurt himself seriously.

Other agents of death were much more efficient. Influenza reached epidemic proportions from Constantinople to Chicago and from Russia came chilling stories of an even worse scourge, cholera. It was said that those infected were buried alive in mass graves and, as a result, those who had not yet contracted the disease were understandably rising up in desperation and being cut down by sabres.

In France, however, the greatest threat of all seemed to come from the anarchist terrorists. Some of them had been seized and convicted for outrages perpetrated during the previous year and now the leaders of the movement ordered a new campaign of terror against the judges. Two had their Paris homes blown up. The year 1892 was bringing to light in France, wrote one British journalist, 'not a few symptoms of a relaxed sense of government responsibility, of weakness in the maintenance of order, and of intensified social hatred'.

THE ANARCHIST THREAT

The police had some successes. More than a hundred anarchists were arrested and a bomb-making factory was uncovered, as well as a plot to poison food in the restaurants of

Gerry Clyde/Michael Holford Library

Excavations at Delphi
The temple at Delphi, on Mount Parnassus in Greece, was dedicated to Apollo, and was believed by the Ancient Greeks to be the centre of the world. The temple, dating from the 4th century BC, fell into decay with the advent of Christianity. In 1892 the French school of archaeology began excavations at Delphi, and much of the site has now been restored.

Anarchist outrages
(left) Terrorist attacks by anarchists reached their height in Paris during 1892. The anarchists believed that organized government was a form of repression, so they aimed their attacks at government representatives or the forces of law and order. This picture shows a bomb exploding in the police headquarters.

The Panama Canal Scandal
(below) Ferdinand de Lesseps, successful engineer of the Suez Canal, enters a police van on his way to prison for corruption, after his new scheme had collapsed.

Archiv für Kunst und Geschichte

the capital. Finally, at the end of March, Ravachol, the most notorious anarchist leader of all, was arrested at a café in the Boulevard Magenta. The anarchists said Ravachol had been betrayed to the police by Véry, the café proprietor, and blew him up with his café. Véry was given a funeral at public expense and the Prime Minister made a speech at the graveside, but this did little to refute charges of weakness. By now judges and juries, it was said, were too fearful to convict anarchists.

CHURCH VERSUS STATE

However atrocious the anarchist crimes might seem, they did not really warrant fears of civil war. They were after all essentially a threat from outside society, against which all

Frenchmen could unite. Other manifestations of violence, though less deadly, were ultimately more damaging because they divided the nation. This was especially true of the conflict between the state and the Catholic church, which reached fever pitch in 1892.

It was ironic that the year in which Monet began to paint his serene studies of Rouen cathedral should also have been the year in which this and other great churches were turned into battlefields. At Nancy the cathedral was torn apart and chairs hurled through the air when part of the congregation took exception to a highly political sermon by the bishop. Similar scenes took place all over the country, as priests staged anti-republican demonstrations in their churches. The Pope produced an encyclical warning the French clergy that they

Cholera epidemic in Russia
In 1892 a serious outbreak of cholera was brought to Russia, apparently, by Muslim pilgrims returning from Mecca. Soldiers destroyed whole villages in an attempt to control the disease. The composer Peter Tchaikovsky (1840-1893) died in the epidemic, as a result of drinking unboiled water.

Mary Evans Picture Library

The Mansell Collection

Switchboard operators
The first telephone exchange opened in London in 1879, and by 1892 the first automatic switchboard was in use. The Scots-born inventor of the telephone, Alexander Graham Bell, had demonstrated his system to Queen Victoria herself, whose enthusiasm encouraged the Post Office to adopt it.

Labour's first MP
James Keir Hardie (1856-1915) entered the House of Commons in 1892 as the first Labour MP. He wore a deerstalker hat for the occasion, which became his symbol. Born in Scotland, he was working in a coal mine by the age of 10, and at 24 he was blacklisted for his union activities. He died aged 59, disillusioned by Labour's decision to support the Great War.

must respect their republican government, but they did not take very much notice of him.

The year was an important one for republicans because it was the centenary of the downfall of the French monarchy and of the setting up of the first French Republic in 1792. An attempt to celebrate 10 August, the day on which Louis XVI had been driven from his palace, was a dismal failure. But when it came to 22 September, the day on which the first Republic had actually been proclaimed, the civic authorities in Paris forced the national government to agree to a grand fête, with processions and illuminations and commemorative addresses. And because the Republic of 1792 had been born out of war, the centenary was also marked by military manoeuvres.

By this time many traditionalist Frenchmen had come to feel that it would be no bad thing if the soldiers were used to back up the forces of law and order, even if it did increase the risk of civil war. After a particularly ugly miner's strike, there was widespread condemnation of government weakness. And when the new session of the Chamber of Deputies opened, the ministry found itself under attack.

PANAMA CANAL SCANDAL

Trouble centred on the affairs of a company formed some years before to cut a canal through the Panama isthmus. Rumours of corruption had long been circulating and, shortly before the Chamber met, an anti-Semitic newspaper ran a story to the effect that the Panama Company had been bribing deputies

Reg Wilson

The Nutcracker Suite
Tchaikovsky's last work for the stage was first performed on 7 December 1892 in St Petersburg (now Leningrad). The ballet was not choreographed well and was only moderately successful. Here Rudolf Nureyev partners Merle Park as the Sugar Plum Fairy in a recent performance of the ballet.

National Museum of Labour History

VOTE FOR

Home Rule.

Democratic Government.

Justice to Labour

No Monopoly.

No Landlordism

Temperance Reform.

Healthy Homes.

Fair Rents.

Eight-Hour Day.

Work for the Unemployed.

KEIR HARDIE.

through the medium of a Jewish financier, the Baron de Reinach. Two days before the Chamber debated the matter, Reinach was found dead and his associate, Cornelius Herz, fled the country.

And the scandal went deeper still. The real division in the Chamber, cried the right-wing deputy who opened the debate, was not between the government and the opposition, but between those who had accepted bribes and those who had not. More than three million francs was alleged to have been distributed. Suffering defeat after defeat in the Chamber, ending with a successful demand for the exhumation of Reinach's body, the government resigned.

But the ministry which finally took office after a week of crisis was merely a reshuffled version of a previous government. Almost immediately the Minister of Finance was forced to resign because of new charges. Shortly before Christmas, the authorities finally gave up any further attempt to protect the directors of the Panama Company, who were thrown into prison.

Only the veteran Ferdinand de Lesseps, the most distinguished engineer in France, creator of both the Suez and the Panama canals, was spared. Unfortunately, further revelations made necessary the imprisonment of France's other great engineer, Gustave Eiffel, designer of the Eiffel Tower. The anarchists did try to make a come-back, by setting off a bomb at the police headquarters in Paris, but the truth was that they had been upstaged: with scapegoats as eminent as Eiffel, the French public no longer had need of them.

Gold in Australia

Gold was discovered in west Australia in 1892, when diggers unearthed large nuggets close to the surface – including the 'Welcome Stranger', weighing 2520 oz. Gold production declined after 1903, because the easily worked deposits were soon exhausted.

Ta-ra-ra-boom-de-ay!

A star performer of the music hall, Lottie Collins made her name in 1892 with the song 'ta-ra-ra-boom-de-ay'. Naughty songs were popular with London audiences.

Der Digger in Australien.

1841-1919

Pierre-Auguste Renoir created some of the most charming paintings of Impressionist art. Trained as a porcelain painter in a small Paris factory, he made the transition from artisan to artist at the age of 19. Throughout his long career, and despite many changes of style, his paintings always remained joyful. They evoke a dreamy, carefree world full of light and colour where beautiful women dance with their lovers.

After struggling for more than 15 years – his Impressionist canvases were derided by the critics – Renoir made his name as a society portrait painter when he was nearly 40. Around this time he married and settled into a happy family life. Later he became crippled by rheumatism and moved south to the Riviera, where he spent his final years painting every day until his death at the age of 78.

The Friendly Impressionist

During his long life, Renoir made many loyal friends, from Claude Monet – the leader of the Impressionists – to his patrons Victor Chocquet and the Charpentier family.

Pierre-Auguste Renoir was born at Limoges in mid-France on 25 February 1841, the fourth of his parents' five children. His father Léonard was a tailor; his mother, Marguerite, a seamstress. The family moved to Paris when Renoir was aged four so he grew up in the capital – at first in a run-down apartment in the courtyard of the Louvre, which was then still a royal palace.

The Renoir household was crowded and hardworking, but the boy had a happy childhood distinguished by the discovery that he had a beautiful voice. The composer Gounod proposed to arrange a complete musical education for him, with a place in the chorus of the Paris Opera. But even at 13, Renoir somehow felt that he was not 'made for that sort of thing'. Instead, he took up another offer – he became an apprentice decorative painter in a small porcelain factory.

Aspiring painter
The young Renoir worked for several years as a decorative painter in a Paris porcelain factory. But at the age of 19 he made the decision to become an artist.

The forest of Fontainebleau
Renoir's art teacher encouraged his students to make trips to the Forest of Fontainebleau, 40 miles south of Paris, and paint in the open air. Renoir stayed there for weeks at a time, spending the days painting the effects of dappled light beneath the great beeches and oaks.

Office National des Forets/J.P. Chasseau

Key Dates

1841 born in Limoges

1844 moves to Paris

1854 apprenticed as porcelain painter

1862 enrols in Charles Gleyre's studio; meets Bazille, Monet and Sisley

1863 paints in Forest of Fontainebleau

1865 meets Lise Tréhot

1870 Franco-Prussian war; Bazille killed

1874 takes part in first Impressionist exhibition

1879 exhibits *Madame Charpentier and her Children*; launched as a society portrait painter

1880 meets Aline Charigot

1881 paints *Luncheon of the Boating Party*; visits Algeria, Spain and Italy

1882 returns to Paris and marries Aline

1885 birth of Pierre, first of three sons

1894 Gabrielle Renard arrives to help Aline

1897 first attack of crippling rheumatism

1903 moves to Riviera

1907 buys last home, Les Collettes

1915 Aline dies

1919 dies at Cagnes

Renoir/The Inn of Mother Anthony/National Museum, Stockholm

Auguste proved so skilful at the job that he was nick-named Mr Rubens and was soon given the task of painting profiles of Marie-Antoinette on the fine white cups. He earned a good living at his craft for five years, before the job of hand-painting was made obsolete by the invention of a mechanical stamping process. It was his first real contact with 'the machine', and turned him against mass-production and standardization for life.

VISITS TO THE LOUVRE

During his time at the factory, Renoir would visit the art galleries of the Louvre during his lunch hours. His great loves were the exquisite 18th century pictures of courtly gaiety painted by Watteau, Boucher and Fragonard, and the dramatic, colourful canvases of Delacroix. But as he told his son Jean, he was most inspired by a superb 16th-century sculpture, the Fountain of the Innocents. And after a year spent painting blinds and a series of murals for cafés, he decided to become an artist.

In 1862, at the age of 21, Renoir became a student at the studio of Charles Gleyre, a very well-known private art school in Paris. Though academic and traditional in character, it gave him an excellent training with plenty of time to go to the Louvre and study the Old Masters. But Gleyre also stressed the importance of sketching out-of-doors, and encouraged him to visit the Forest of Fontainebleau. This feature of Gleyre's teaching and his remarkable group of young art students had a profound effect on Renoir's career.

Among the students were Claude Monet, Alfred Sisley and Frédéric Bazille, through whom

Mother Anthony's Inn
During his visits to Fontainebleau, Renoir often stayed at this inn in the tiny village of Marlotte. In 1866, he painted his friends there: Monet (reaching for his tobacco), Sisley (in a hat) and Jules LeCoeur.

Renoir met Edgar Degas and Edouard Manet, as well as many leading writers and critics. Together they gradually forged a close-knit group that met regularly in the Paris cafés to discuss their theories, and the ideas of Impressionism emerged.

Working closely with Monet in the Forest of Fontainebleau (a two-day walk from Paris), Renoir gradually developed his own style. But their collaboration reached a climax in the summer of 1869 when, working together at the popular river-

Renoir's Model Mistress

Renoir met Lise Tréhot when he was in his early twenties and she was just 16: her sister lived with Renoir's friend and fellow-artist Jules LeCoeur in Marlotte village.

The artist was attracted by the young girl's dark, pretty features and rounded figure. She soon became his favourite model – and mistress. He painted her more than 20 times between 1865 and 1872: in that year, the couple parted and Lise married. She never saw Renoir again.

Teenage girlfriend
(left) This photograph of Lise was taken around the time that she and Renoir met.

Oriental temptress
Renoir delighted in painting Lise in different guises. In The Odalisque *(below) he painted her as an Algerian harem-girl with an inviting look in her eye. Her exotic, sumptuous dress and openly seductive pose are a far cry from the demure post-master's daughter in the photograph.*

Renoir/Odalisque/National Gallery, Washington

109

side restaurant known as La Grenouillère, the two men produced the canvases which are now regarded as the first Impressionist paintings.

These were days of financial hardship for both men. Renoir at least had some help from his family, and took bread and scraps for Monet from his table. But neither had cash to spare for paint or canvas. It was only money from Bazille, who had a small private income, which kept them going.

RENOIR IN THE CAVALRY

In 1870, this period of intense creativity was brought to an abrupt halt by the Franco-Prussian War. Renoir was called up, and found himself training horses for the cavalry in the Pyrenees, far from the fighting. He returned to Paris in the middle of the bitter Commune battle of 1871, but was lucky enough to have influential friends on both sides who made it possible for him to travel in and out of the city.

Renoir continued to paint and the group slowly reformed, though without Bazille, who had been killed in the war. Through Monet, Renoir now met Paul Durand-Ruel, the first art-dealer to support the Impressionists, who agreed to take his work. Soon he was selling enough to move into a large studio in the Rue St Georges. After a sequence of garret studios over the years, he now laughingly declared he had 'arrived'.

This studio, which he occupied for over ten years, became an important meeting place for the Impressionist group and its associates. Renoir's younger brother Edmond, who had emerged as a leading writer and art critic, lived downstairs and made the studio almost too much of a meeting

Influential friends and patrons
(left) This painting of Madame Charpentier and her Children *made Renoir's name as a society portrait painter when it was exhibited at the 1879 Salon. The woman in the picture was the wife of the publisher Georges Charpentier, and it was through her husband's influence that the painting was exhibited.*

After the exhibition, a band of enthusiastic collectors grew up among the Parisian élite. The most important was the diplomat Paul Bérard. He owned over 30 Renoirs, many of which were painted during the artist's visits to the Bérard's country house at Wargemont, near Dieppe (above).

Renoir/Madame Charpentier and her Children/Metropolitan Museum of Art, New York

Journey to Algeria
(below) Renoir travelled to Algeria in 1881, and then went on to study the Old Masters in Spain and Italy. It was a pivotal year for him both personally and artistically: on his return to Paris, he married, and adopted a new 'harsh' style of painting.

place. Renoir was forced at times to seek small studios for the peace he needed to work.

Skinny, bearded and immensely charming, with a nervous, modest manner, Renoir inspired extraordinary affection among his friends. Although not demonstrative – he hated any public show of emotion – he showed intense loyalty and love with acts of quiet generosity. One of his life-long friends, the artist Paul Cézanne, was the complete opposite. Where Cézanne was suspicious of people, Renoir would not waste his energy worrying about being exploited. 'People love to be nice,' he said, 'but you must give them the chance.'

Even with the new studio, Renoir's money problems were far from over. During the 1870s Renoir's work, like that of other Impressionist

A city in revolt
(above) After France's defeat by the Germans, angry Parisians rebelled against their Republican government and formed a Commune. These were bloody days, and Renoir was once arrested as a spy, only to be saved from the firing squad by one of the Commune leaders whom he had once protected. He also had influential friends on the Republican side: while others were kept in or out of the city, Renoir passed freely between Communist Paris and Republican France.

Pretty young wife
(right) This detail from Dance in the Country (1883) *shows Renoir's young wife Aline around the time of their marriage.*

Renoir/Dance in the Country/Musée d'Orsay, Paris

painters, was ignored or ridiculed by the academic critics – one of his nudes was once compared to a 'mass of rotting flesh'. But gradually, a small and devoted band of enthusiasts developed.

One of them, Victor Chocquet, became a particular admirer and proceeded to form a considerable collection of Renoir's work. This gave the painter enormous confidence at a difficult time, but on its own it was not enough to support him. He was still dependent on portrait commissions gained via the Salon, until enlightened middle-class families like the Charpentiers and the Bérards became his patrons, enabling him to continue with the more experimental Parisian scenes.

Through all these years Renoir had remained a bachelor. There had been romances, probably including one with Lise Tréhot whom he painted so often in the 1860s, but Renoir seems always to have regarded the idea of marriage and children as a distraction from the focus of his life – painting.

But around the age of 40, he met Aline Charigot, a pretty girl some 20 years younger than himself, who had occasionally modelled for him. Their relationship developed during the summer of 1881, while he was working on the great masterpiece of his Impressionist period, *The Luncheon of the Boating Party*, for which she was one of the

Renoir and his family
Renoir enjoyed a settled family life with his wife Aline and their three sons. Aline's cousin Gabrielle (on the right) helped with the children and became Renoir's favourite model.

models. He taught her to swim, and they danced and went boating together. The gentle Aline had almond eyes and 'she walked on the grass without hurting it', but though they loved each other, their affair was not to be straightforward.

Renoir was at a crisis in his painting. Despite Aline's suggestion that they should go and stay in her small home village in Burgundy, he was reluctant to leave Paris and equally reluctant to have children. Aline called things off. Renoir started to travel intensively: first to Normandy, then Algeria, a country he associated with Delacroix, then to Spain and Italy to see the works of the Old Masters – Velázquez in Madrid, Titian in Venice, and Raphael in Rome – and the murals at Pompeii.

A WIFE AND CHILDREN

But Renoir did not forget Aline, and returned to Paris to marry her. It was to be a marriage of harmony and happiness. She brought him peace of mind as well as children whom he could paint and, as he put it, 'Time to think. She kept an atmosphere of activity around me exactly suited to my needs and concerns.'

Back in his old Rue St Georges studio, Renoir absorbed the visual impressions of his travels into a new way of painting. The so-called 'harsh' style he developed first created further difficulties for his dealer, and it was only the huge enthusiasm of Americans for his work from 1885 that enabled Renoir to support his wife and newly-born son Pierre in reasonable comfort.

Though not yet rich, he was able to move with his family to a larger house in Montmartre and to take on help for Aline. Gabrielle Renard, a distant cousin of Aline's, arrived in 1894. Aged just 15, she had never before left the village of Essones in Burgundy where she and Aline were born. The rosy-skinned, dark-haired young girl soon became part of the family, helping to bring up the younger sons Jean and Claude, and frequently posed as a model.

Renoir enjoyed family life, working hard – and by now selling well – seeing friends every Saturday night, when Aline would hold 'open-house', and visiting his mother on Sundays. But disaster was soon to strike in the form of a serious illness. In 1897, he broke his arm falling off a bicycle, and this brought on the first attack of the muscular rheumatism that slowly started to cripple him and

The final years
(above) Renoir, aged about 64 and suffering from rheumatism, sits painting in his garden in the south of France. He moved there for his health, but although the beauty of the place inspired a flood of creativity, his illness crippled him.

Portrait of a Composer

Towards the end of his months of travel in Spain and Italy, Renoir visited Richard Wagner at his home in Sicily in January 1882. He was not a fan of Wagner, whose music he found boring, but his friend Judge Lascoux had commissioned him to paint the composer. Granted only a brief interview, Renoir completed Wagner's portrait in just over half an hour. The two men did not take to each other. Renoir continued to prefer the light opera and easy company of his neighbour, Jacques Offenbach.

Richard Wagner
Renoir painted this portrait in just 35 minutes on January 15 1882 – the date appears on the left. The composer thought the picture made him look like a protestant minister.

Renoir/Wagner/Musée d'Orsay, Paris

he continued to paint virtually non-stop, only halting briefly at Aline's death in 1915.

In his last years, Renoir took up sculpture – with two young sculptors acting as his hands, since his own were too crippled to use. The fact that these sculptures are unmistakably Renoir's bears witness to his exceptional ability to communicate.

Renoir painted to the end, working in a special glass studio in his garden. He was carried there daily in his sedan chair, always wearing his white out-of-doors hat, and placed in his wheelchair. Gabrielle would push the paintbrush between his twisted fingers. One day, after Renoir had painted some anemones a maid had brought him, he asked a friend to take his brush, saying 'I think I am beginning to understand something about it.' He died later that night, on 3 December 1919.

The French Riviera
Renoir built his last home, Les Collettes, on a piece of land outside Cagnes on the French Riviera.

Renoir's famous son
Renoir's second son Jean became famous as the director of numerous films. His biography Renoir, My Father *is full of fascinating anecdotes which bring to life the painter's charming personality.*

never left him free from pain for the rest of his life. By enormous force of will, aided by the devotions of Aline, Gabrielle and their friends, he somehow continued to paint.

To relieve the pain, Renoir spent increasingly long periods in the warmth of the South of France. In 1907, he built a beautiful house in Cagnes on the Riviera. With its many olive trees and orange blossom, and its views over the Mediterranean, 'Les Collettes' became his base for painting. The brilliant light and relaxed atmosphere helped ease his muscular pain and released a flood of creativity in a colourful, classical style.

However, the beauty of the place could not cure rheumatism. By 1908 Renoir could only walk with sticks. By 1912, his arms and legs were crippled and he was confined to a wheelchair. Nonetheless

Painting for Pleasure

**For Renoir, painting was a way of expressing his pleasure in life.
He always enjoyed portraying his friends and lovers, and was never
ashamed of making pretty pictures.**

'Why shouldn't art be pretty?' Renoir asked once. 'There are enough unpleasant things in the world.' This simple statement sums up his attitude to both life and painting – he had a tremendous capacity for enjoyment, and his art was an expression of his pleasure in life. Renoir only worked when he felt happy, and he deliberately chose subjects that he considered attractive: lush landscapes, fruit and flowers, people enjoying themselves, children playing and, above all, beautiful women.

Nothing gave him greater pleasure than painting women, and although our idea of fashionable beauty may have changed considerably since Renoir's time, the young women we see in his paintings still evoke an era when living in Paris was fun. He was brought up the son of a tailor in the centre of the city, and his models are invariably working girls – seamstresses, milliners, actresses – who, he once said, had the precious gift of living for the moment.

Natural as it seems now, Renoir's choice of subject matter was radical and daring when he decided at the age of 21 to enrol as an art student at the studio of Charles Gleyre. The Paris art world was still dominated by the official Salon, which

Success as a portrait painter
(below) Renoir earned much of his money by painting portraits on commission. In 1876 he painted his patron, the customs official Victor Chocquet.

preferred to exhibit works on historical and literary themes, painted in a realistic style. Only in the past few years had younger artists, notably Gustave Courbet, turned to everyday subjects which were more expressive of a fast-changing France.

Renoir quickly found that he was more interested in life on the street corner than in the usual studio practice of copying plaster casts of antique sculpture. His teacher could not persuade him that the big toe of a Roman consul should be any more majestic than the toe of a local coal man. One day, exasperated with his pupil, Gleyre said, 'No doubt you took up painting just to amuse yourself. And Renoir replied, 'Certainly. If it didn't amuse me I wouldn't be doing it.'

THE IMPRESSIONIST YEARS

While studying at Gleyre's studio, Renoir became friendly with a group of fellow students, dominated by the dynamic personality of Claude Monet, who were later to become famous as the Impressionists. Together they went on painting trips to the Forest of Fontainebleau, 40 miles south of Paris, where they worked out in the open air. Renoir, very impressed by Courbet, used subdued browns and blacks in his work. But one day the artist Narcisse Diaz chanced upon him in the forest and, examining Renoir's canvas, asked 'Why the devil do you paint in such dark colours?'

Le Moulin de la Galette (1876)
This painting of a café shows a favourite subject – his friends enjoying themselves.

The Bathers (1884-87)
Renoir always loved painting nudes. This picture, with its hard outlines, illustrates his 'harsh' style.

Private Collection

Philadelphia Museum of Art

Musée d'Orsay, Paris

Musée d'Orsay, Paris

This encouraged Renoir to use the lighter, rainbow colours he instinctively preferred and which he had learned to handle during his early years as a porcelain painter.

During the late 1860s, Monet and Renoir worked very closely together, for they were both attracted by sparkling river scenes and views of bustling Paris. Several of their pictures at this time are of almost identical scenes, but Renoir's style is softer and more delicate than Monet's. Working out of doors, where the light could not be controlled as in a studio, they had to paint quickly to capture the colours in nature before they changed – for

Flower paintings
(above) In paintings like Moss Roses (c. 1880) *Renoir discovered a wonderful form of relaxation: 'I just let my brain rest when I paint flowers', he said. In the 1890s, he painted many still-lifes of roses, experimenting with the same flesh tints he used for his nudes.*

Private Collection

Musée Renoir

Preparatory drawings
Precise drawings, like this sketch for Dance in the Country (1883), *are rare in Renoir's work before the 1880s.*

The heat of Algeria
(above) Following two trips to Algeria, where he painted The Steps (1882) *Renoir's colours became noticeably 'hotter'.*

Venus Victrix
In his last years, although crippled by rheumatism, Renoir created many sculptures with the help of assistants.

115

Giraudon

Musée d'Orsay, Paris

example, when clouds covered the sun. So they made no attempt to blend their brushstrokes in the traditional way. Instead they placed different colours side by side, in the manner soon to be generally described as Impressionist.

Renoir enjoyed painting landscapes, but he was always more interested in people. Throughout his life he included his friends and lovers in his pictures – initially, as a penniless artist, they were the only models available to him. Some of their faces are distinctively 'Renoir', with almond-shaped eyes and luxuriant hair, but what he looked for especially in a model was 'an air of serenity' and a good skin that 'took the light'. Some of Renoir's most successful early works are portraits, and his graceful, gentle style was particularly suited to painting children.

During his Impressionist years, Renoir developed a fascination with the effect of light passing through foliage to fall as dappled shadows on the ground, and on human forms. In his painting *Le Moulin de la Galette*, a large, complex composition, Renoir used the light passing through the trees to unite his figures with their surroundings. Although Renoir painted this work in his studio, he visited its location – a Montmartre dance-hall –

The Swing (1876)

(above) Renoir painted this picture out-of-doors, in the shady garden of his studio in Montmartre. He used bright blue for the shadows and yellow and pink for the pools of dappled sunlight. By contrasting cool with warm colours, he was able to suggest the brilliance of a sunny day. Renoir also used blue for the bows on the woman's pink dress (detail right), across which blue shadows dance. Behind, dots of light break up the blue shadow on the path into a rich pattern.

Favourite colours

Renoir's hand-written list of the colours he used shows that he favoured two kinds of blue – Cobalt Blue and Ultramarine.

COMPARISONS

Pictures of Women

Painters have always enjoyed painting women, whether nude or fully clothed, but different generations have had different ideas about how they should be portrayed. Boucher's sensual nudes, painted in the 18th century, were admired because they were 'ideal' women masquerading as classical nymphs and goddesses. But Courbet's 'real' women, with their commonplace features and contemporary dress, were considered vulgar by the 19th-century critics. Renoir admired Courbet's realism but he also loved what he termed the 'racy and dignified' women who inhabited Boucher's artificial world.

Petit Palais, Paris

The Louvre, Paris

François Boucher (1703-70) Diana Bathing
This painting was one of Renoir's favourites – he copied the design for a porcelain service. He shared Boucher's delight in painting soft skin. In later years, Renoir painted numerous pictures of nudes bathing.

Gustave Courbet (1819-77) Young Women on the Banks of the Seine
Courbet's straightforward and simple treatment of a scene from everyday life had a special appeal for Renoir. He admired the robustness of the figures, the extravagance of their dress and the brilliant summer landscape.

every day, immersing himself in the life of the area and making sketches on the spot.

Throughout the 1870s Renoir exhibited regularly with the Impressionists, but he also submitted paintings to the Salon. He was always more traditional than the other Impressionists and never for a moment considered himself a revolutionary. While his anarchist friend, the painter Camille Pissarro, wanted to burn down the Louvre, Renoir was a frequent visitor to the gallery.

A CHANGE OF STYLE

At first he saw no contradiction between his Impressionist insistence on painting directly from nature and his reverent study of Old Masters. But in 1883, following a trip to Italy, Renoir was no longer able to reconcile the two. He told a friend: 'I had travelled as far as Impressionism could take me and I realized that I could neither paint nor draw.' Subsequently, Renoir dramatically changed his style, and developed a 'harsh' technique, surrounding his figures with hard, sinuous outlines. In *The Bathers* (1884) he adopted the Old Masters' method of making detailed preparatory drawings. The resulting work is as flat and decorative as a mural at Pompeii.

By the 1890s, these harsh outlines had melted again as Renoir returned to a style more in harmony with his instincts. He began to use warmer colours, especially reds – possibly as a result of two earlier trips to Algeria where he had been most impressed by the hot, sultry light. He painted his children, their beautiful, robust nurse Gabrielle, and a variety of large, sensual nudes, all glowing with radiant colour.

Renoir also did a number of flower paintings, in which he experimented with the same rosy flesh tints he used for his nudes. And at the end of his life, when his hands were increasingly crippled by rheumatism, Renoir began to execute small bronze sculptures with the help of studio assistants. These solid, rounded figures were yet another expression of his endless delight in the human form. 'I never think,' he said, 'that I have finished a nude, until I feel that I could pinch it.'

THE MAKING OF A MASTERPIECE

The Luncheon of the Boating Party

Renoir began work on the *Luncheon of the Boating Party* (see pp.124-5) in the summer of 1881. It was a subject that he had been 'itching' to paint for some time – a merry group of friends lunching on the terrace of the Restaurant Fournaise at the Isle of Chatou on the River Seine. A friend named Baron Barbier, a good-natured regimental captain who much preferred horses to paintings, volunteered to stage-manage the affair – rounding up all Renoir's friends and even making sure the boats were properly positioned for the background. Then Renoir began to make studies and sketches on the spot. The result is an Impressionist masterpiece, filled with a spirit of 'joie de vivre'. But the picture marked the end of an era. Shortly afterwards Renoir changed his style.

Boats on the Seine
(right) The boats glimpsed in the background remind us that the friends relaxing over lunch have just returned from the river.

Renoir's future wife
(below) This young woman, shown in a remarkably natural pose, is Aline Charigot, Renoir's wife-to-be. The Restaurant Fournaise was their favourite meeting place at the time.

The Restaurant Fournaise
(above) Sunday-trippers flocked to this restaurant near Chatou. They ate out on the first-floor terrace overlooking the Seine.

Still-life
(right) Renoir's skill as a painter is shown in this sparkling still-life. The bottles and glasses take on all the colours of the objects around them.

The Bridgeman Art Library

Phillips Collection, Washington

> 'The Impressionists reach the summit of their art when they paint our French Sundays.'
>
> French critic

Friends Around the Table

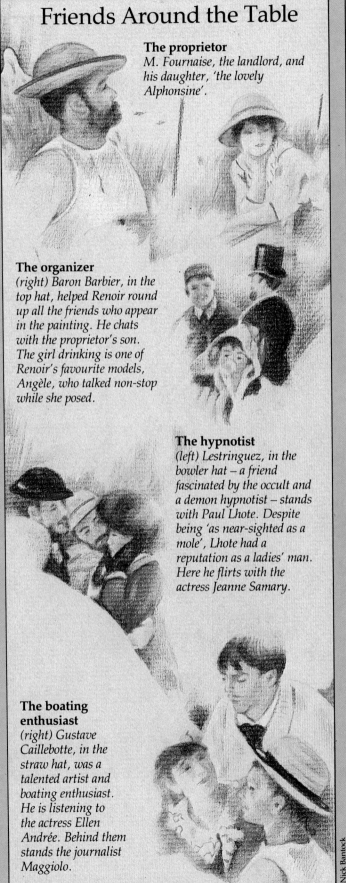

The proprietor
M. Fournaise, the landlord, and his daughter, 'the lovely Alphonsine'.

The organizer
(right) Baron Barbier, in the top hat, helped Renoir round up all the friends who appear in the painting. He chats with the proprietor's son. The girl drinking is one of Renoir's favourite models, Angèle, who talked non-stop while she posed.

The hypnotist
(left) Lestringuez, in the bowler hat – a friend fascinated by the occult and a demon hypnotist – stands with Paul Lhote. Despite being 'as near-sighted as a mole', Lhote had a reputation as a ladies' man. Here he flirts with the actress Jeanne Samary.

The boating enthusiast
(right) Gustave Caillebotte, in the straw hat, was a talented artist and boating enthusiast. He is listening to the actress Ellen Andrée. Behind them stands the journalist Maggiolo.

Nick Bantock

Gallery

Renoir's sparkling picture of La Grenouillère – a popular bathing place on the River Seine – was one of his first pictures in the new Impressionist style. He went on to exhibit La Loge at the first Impressionist Exhibition in 1874, and returned to its theatrical theme two years later in The First Night Out. Such scenes of Parisian life and sunny views of the

La Grenouillère *1869*
26″ × 32″ Nationalmuseum, Stockholm

Renoir and his friend Claude Monet both painted views of La Grenouillère, the popular bathing place on the Seine. Working in the open air, they set up their easels side by side, to paint the lively crowds and the reflections on the water.

River Seine – like the girls boating in The Skiff – were favourite subjects for many of the Impressionists.

But the Luncheon of the Boating Party, in which many of Renoir's friends can be seen, marked a water-shed in his career. Soon afterwards, he began to paint pictures like the famous Umbrellas, and Dance in the Town, in a more severe 'harsh' style. At this time he also painted some beautiful still lifes, like the colourful Fruits of the Midi. Towards the end of his life, Renoir painted predominantly nudes. After the Bath, with its warm, melting colours and the subject's full curves, is a fine example of the 'hot' style of his last years.

La Loge *1874*
31½″ × 25″ Courtauld Institute Galleries, London

Renoir's younger brother Edmond and a model called Nini posed for this picture in Renoir's studio. Nini was dressed up to look like a wealthy woman at the opera. The painting was bought by a dealer for 425 francs, which Renoir already owed in rent.

The First Night Out *c.1876/7*
25½″ × 20″ National Gallery, London

*In this magical painting, Renoir captured the wide-eyed excitement
and nervous anticipation of a young girl on her first visit to the
theatre. In her eagerness she leans forward, clasping her bouquet
of flowers. The audience is painted in broad, sketchy brushstrokes
and their blurred faces suggest the movement of their heads.*

The Skiff *c.1879*
28″ × 36″ National Gallery, London

Renoir painted The Skiff *on a hazy summer's day at Asnières,
concentrating on the glistening effect of sunlight on moving water.
The contrasting colours, yellow-orange for the boat and bright blue for
the water, contribute to the vibrancy of the scene. In the background,
the steam-train from Paris is puffing through the landscape.*

Luncheon of the Boating Party *1881*
50″ × 69″ The Phillips Collection, Washington DC

This famous picture – which captures the lazy atmosphere of a perfect French Sunday – was painted on the terrace of the restaurant at La Grenouillère. (The restaurant can be seen on the right in Renoir's earlier painting, La Grenouillère, on page 120.) Renoir's friends posed for him under the awning, with the warm sunlight filtering through.

Fruits of the Midi *1881*
20″ × 27″ Art Institute of Chicago

Renoir painted many still-lifes of fruit and flowers. In this picture he selected fruits and vegetables that would lend themselves to a wonderful colour arrangement – among them red pimentos, purple-blue aubergines and yellow-green lemons.

Dance in the Town *1883*
71″ × 35½″ Musée d'Orsay, Paris

*In 1883 Renoir was commissioned to paint a pair of pictures
contrasting the lifestyles of the town and the country. In this 'town'
painting, the cool colours, impersonal setting and elegant dress of the
dancers illustrate the sophisticated manners of well-to-do Parisians.*

The Umbrellas *c.1881-6*
71″ × 45″ National Gallery, London

*In this famous picture, a Paris crowd braves
the showers under a canopy of open umbrellas.*

Sotheby's, London

After the Bath *c.1888*
25½" × 21¼" Private Collection, Japan

*In his later years, Renoir's favourite subject was the nude. He painted
hundreds in rich, glowing colours, revelling in their roundness and
fullness of form. 'My concern,' he said 'has always been to paint nudes
as if they were some splendid fruit.'*

Sundays in the Country

Renoir's famous paintings of his friends at play – dancing, boating, eating, chatting – are a celebration of French summer outings. Every Sunday, thousands of day-trippers took the train out of Paris for pleasure spots on the banks of the Seine.

For Parisians in the second half of the 19th century, Sunday was the one day that they could forget about work and enjoy themselves. The fresh, unspoilt beauty of the countryside had become increasingly attractive to city-dwellers as their own surroundings became more built-up, and with the coming of the railways, destinations that had previously involved long, arduous journeys were now within easy reach of everyone.

DRESSING UP FOR SUNDAY

'Of course you may have a little recreation on Sunday . . .' wrote one preacher to his readers. And they certainly took him at his word. Sunday outings, especially for the working community, soon became the social highlight of the week. Men and women dressed up in their 'Sunday best', the women wearing their prettiest crinolines and carrying sunshades, and headed for the country.

One of the favourite haunts of day-trippers from

The age of the train
Pleasure-bent Parisians wearing their best clothes board the crowded 'Sunday' train for a trip into the country. The railways – newly built in Renoir's time – gave everyone a chance to escape from the city on their day off.

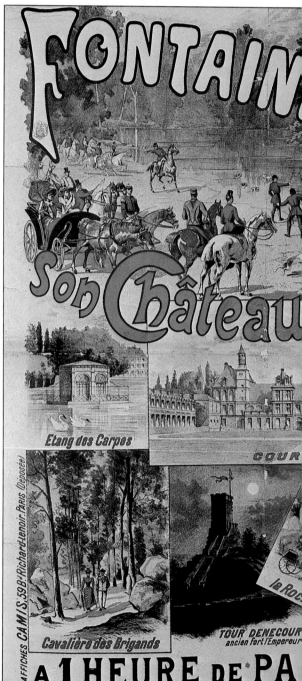

Carnavalet/Bulloz

Lauros-Giraudon

130

Day trips from Paris

The railways carried passengers out of Paris in two directions: northwest to the riverside villages around Argenteuil and southeast to Fontainebleau – 62,000 acres of woodland, with spectacular crags and gorges.

Fontainebleau Palace

The French court took up residence at Fontainebleau for six weeks every spring. The sight of aristocrats picnicking in the forest was an added attraction for the Sunday trippers.

Paris was the Forest of Fontainebleau, lying some 40 miles south of the capital. Before 1849, access to Fontainebleau had been difficult, requiring a day-long journey by stage-coach which had to be booked several days in advance. But in August of that year a new railway line opened. Now it took just 90 minutes to reach Melun, at the edge of the woods, and Parisians flocked there to take advantage of the various attractions of the region.

The rugged scenery of the place, with its outcrop of craggy rocks and still untamed woodland, had nurtured a whole generation of landscape painters, succeeded now by younger artists – among them Renoir and Monet – who delighted in open-air painting. The little villages of Barbizon and Chailly, situated on the north-east borders of the forest, were particular favourites with artists, being just a short walk from some spectacular scenery: centuries-old beeches and oaks lining the road at Chailly and the rocky gorges of Apremont. The grotesque shapes of some of the rocks had given rise to stories that the forest was inhabited by fantastic monsters. Its woodland had also acquired a romantic reputation as the hideout of escaped convicts and brigands.

Sunday trippers would trek the five miles to Barbizon from Melun Station, or take a gig if they were lucky enough to get one. Shop-assistants,

Delights of Fontainebleau

(left) A poster advertises the palace and forest at Fontainebleau – a 90-minute ride from the Gare de Lyon station in Paris. The line, built in 1849, went to Melun, from where visitors could walk or take a gig to Chailly, Barbizon, Fontainebleau and other villages.

A family picnic

A photograph dated 1888 shows a family enjoying a game of whist after their picnic lunch – washed down with liberal quantities of wine.

Giraudon

The Seine at Argenteuil
(left) A railway poster promotes the delights of Argenteuil, northwest of Paris. The tranquil village soon attracted artists – Claude Monet set up a studio in a houseboat, and Renoir too enjoyed painting by the Seine.

clerks, apprentices and students would gather here – some to sketch; most, out of curiosity, to watch the painters at work; others to picnic and stroll under the trees. On one occasion Renoir was spied by a group of Parisian rowdies who were greatly amused by his old-fashioned artist's smock. They kicked his palette out of his hand, while the girls laughingly poked at him with their parasols. Most of the trippers, however, were interested in more harmless amusements. One Belgian artist noted: 'At present there are crowds of people gathered here, and everywhere exclamations of joy can be heard throughout the forest.'

Rowing parties
(right) The 1880s saw a growing enthusiasm for rowing – both for pleasure and for sport. Regattas, which began in the spring, were competitive events much painted by the Impressionists.

Jean-Loup Charmet

INNS OF THE FOREST

With their reputation for lively, hospitable inns, home to many an artist, Barbizon and Chailly could also provide food, drink and plenty of entertaining conversation. One such inn, the Auberge Ganne at Chailly, had become renowned as an artistic centre. It was not so famous for its culinary delights. The Goncourt brothers, watercolour artists who also kept detailed notebooks, were dismayed by the 'monotony of omelettes' and the 'pewter forks that stained the fingers'. The tiny village of Marlotte, to the south of the forest, was also popular with young painters.

The Fontainebleau region retained its popularity as a sight-seeing spot until the very end of the century. The French court, which took up residence at the Chateau of Fontainebleau for six weeks every spring, would sometimes travel down by coach to picnic in a select corner of the

Jean-Loup Charmet

Bathing at Bougival
(left) For young men, the great attraction of bathing resorts like Bougival was the chance to enjoy wine, women and song. Respectable young ladies were kept well away from such carefree scenes.

Drinks on the terrace
(right) Cafés overlooking the water gave the more restrained visitors a good viewpoint for watching the antics on the river.

woods, providing an added twist of excitement for the Parisian weekenders.

Easier communications between Paris and its surrounding countryside also opened up areas to the north of the city. The River Seine, on its winding course towards the Normandy coast, was dotted with villages and islands which were popular with boating enthusiasts.

In places made famous for us through their association with painters and paintings – Argenteuil, Bougival, Chatou and its island and La Grenouillère (the 'frog pond') – Sunday trippers could indulge in a variety of amusements, from boating and bathing to the sophisticated joys of dancing and drinking in the many *guingettes*, or open-air cafés that lined the river banks.

Situated within 25 minutes by train from Paris's Gare St Lazare, Argenteuil was understandably popular. Today it is a drab suburb of Paris, but in the 1860s and 70s it was still a village, noted for its market gardens and its vineyards.

BOATING ON THE SEINE

The town itself might show the first signs of encroaching industrialization – factory chimneys were already visible – but the riverside at Argenteuil boasted lively *guingettes* from which the sound of the dance music of the day could be heard mingled with the animated chatter of customers, and was a meeting place for sail-boat enthusiasts. 'The taste for boating has developed remarkably in the last 15 years,' wrote an observer of the French scene in 1867. Regattas were a regular event.

Bougival, too, a little further to the west along the river, together with Chatou on the opposite bank, attracted a real mixture of Sunday visitors. The outdoor restaurants and pleasure-boat companies flourished with the trade from boatmen and their ladies, journalists, office workers and the coquettish young women, nicknamed *grenouilles* ('frogs') who thronged there. At Chatou, the Restaurant Fournaise enjoyed years of popularity.

Between these two resorts lay a string of islands running up the middle of the river. Crowds would wait for the ferry to take them across to their favourite islands of La Loge or Croissy, and after a picnic and rest they might perhaps bathe at La Grenouillère nearby. These charming pockets of woodland and water on the Seine were the meeting places of writers and artists as well. The author Guy de Maupassant, who knew and loved the area, has left us a colourful description of the *grenouilles*, 'yellow-haired girls with heavily rouged faces, made-up eyes and excessively red lips . . . in extravagant dresses that trail on the fresh turf.'

These Sunday outings were precious days, when the very real hardships of daily life could briefly be forgotten. For Renoir, they offered a feast of vibrant life – 'a never-ending party, and what a jumble of social sets!' 'How one laughed in those days!' the artist reminisced later. 'Machinery didn't take up the whole of life; there was time for living, and we made the most of it.'

Jean-Loup Charmet

A Year in the Life 1871

Europe was in turmoil that year. Renoir lived in a Paris ringed with armies, where the citizens had revolted against their own Republican government to form a left-wing Commune. Months of hardship and near-starvation ended with a brutal bloodbath. In Italy, nationalist armies marched into Rome to proclaim their new capital. And in Britain there were fears of a German invasion.

Marc Evans Picture Library

Franco-Prussian War
In January 1871 France surrendered to the Germans after a short but bloody war, which ended French dominance in Europe. The Emperor Napoleon III had been defeated at Sedan in 1870, but was then deposed; and the new Third Republic continued the war. When the Germans besieged Paris, the War Minister escaped in a balloon and amassed new troops to continue the futile fight.

The Paris Commune
The harsh terms of the peace treaty with Germany angered the Parisians, who had suffered badly under siege. They rebelled against their own Republican government and set up an independent Commune. Conditions in Paris remained appalling: food was so scarce they were reduced to eating rats. But the revolution failed and Republican troops entered Paris on 21 May 1871.

Georges Goldner

The first day of the year was Sunday. At the Palace of Versailles outside Paris it was marked by a solemn service of praise and thanksgiving in the royal chapel. This was a Roman Catholic chapel, since the kings and emperors of France had always been champions of that faith. But the palace was no longer in French hands, and the service on 1 January 1871 was Protestant – an outrage to all good Catholics, since it was conducted according to German Lutheran rites.

Versailles had become the headquarters of the King of Prussia, whose powerful army had defeated the French in a matter of months and was now laying siege to Paris. A few days into the New Year, the German princes hailed Wilhelm I as their new overlord, Emperor of all Germany. Meanwhile, Napoleon III, who had been Emperor of the French until his surrender at the Battle of Sedan, was deposed in favour of the Third Republic. The new government put up little further resistance, but some troops were organized in the countryside.

THE NEW ITALY

In Rome itself, the seat of papal power for more than 1,000 years, the affront to the Catholic Church was even more dramatic. French troops had been guarding the Pope, but the war against Germany had forced them to withdraw. Now the Italian armies marched in. At long last they had unified their country, and Rome became a civil capital for the new state. 'Many here counsel me to leave Rome,' the Pope cried in desperation, 'but where am I to go? I should have to wander from one country to

The Great Fire of Chicago
The fire broke out on 8 October 1871 – how, nobody knows – and swept through the timber-built city leaving 90,000 homeless and 300 dead. Heavy rain extinguished the blaze after 27 hours of fierce burning.

Charles Darwin
Darwin's Descent of Man, *his second great work on evolution, was published in 1871. This along with* On the Origin of Species *(1859) horrified the Church and Darwin became the butt of much satirical attack. He had dared to suggest that Man was related to the ape.*

Currier & Ives/Great Fire of Chicago

another, and it is very hard for an old man to turn vagabond.'

Old men might fear for the future but the young radicals rejoiced. For months atheists and revolutionaries had held international councils all over Europe, to rival the Pope's Vatican Council in Rome. Now it was time to move from words to action. Revolution, the ultimate challenge to the old order, was at hand.

The outbreak came in March, inside the besieged city of Paris. That winter had been the fiercest in memory, and for ordinary Parisians life had become a nightmare of hunger and cold, of days and nights spent in queues for food and fuel under constant threat of bombardment. With little work to be had, the poor gravitated to revolutionary clubs where there was at least a little warmth and light and companionship. There they were roused to fury by tirades against their bourgeois masters, who still lived in luxury and were said to be plotting to sell the city to the enemy – the Germans.

REVOLUTION IN PARIS

The Republican authorities, now based at Versailles, were indeed trying to come to terms with the Germans. They tried to regain control of Paris by seizing the guns on the heights of Montmartre which dominated the city. When they failed, the soldiers of the National Guard joined the citizens of Paris in proclaiming a Commune, a revolutionary government based on the ideas of Karl Marx. A few days later Communes were also set up in Lyons and Marseilles.

The circus comes to town
In 1871, the entrepreneur P.T. Barnum started his famous circus – The Greatest Show on Earth – in Brooklyn, New York. In the same year, the self-appointed 'Lord' Sanger opened the popular permanent circus named Astley's in England.

The Communes in Lyons and Marseilles collapsed within a matter of days, but in Paris the forces of revolution defied the French government for more than two months. The limit of the Commune's authority, the line between Paris and the rest of France, became the frontier between the existing social order of Europe and a communist future.

CROSSING THE BORDER

Renoir was one of the few people able to cross that frontier, to visit his family and get on with his painting. He had safe conducts both from the Commune and from the Versailles authorities. As he slipped from Republican France into the revolutionary Commune, he hid his Versailles pass in a tree stump, picking it up and hiding the other on his return.

The frontier Renoir crossed so easily was impassable for most people, a dividing line drawn between the forces of good and evil. Throughout Europe the rich and respectable viewed the Communards as the enemies of mankind, devils incarnate. Their challenge, it seemed, was not just to law and order but to God himself. In late May, government forces began to close in on Paris and the Commune authorities ordered the wholesale destruction of property and the shooting of prisoners. Outraged government troops took reprisals and appalling atrocities were perpetrated on both sides before the Commune collapsed.

The humiliation of the French Republic by the German Empire soon had repercussions, especially in England. 'From private sources I know that the military aristocratic caste in

Rasputin

Rasputin, the infamous monk who became the most powerful man in Russia, was born in 1871. His name – meaning 'debauchee' – was given to him as a youth, before he became a 'holy' man and healer. As court favourite to the Empress Alexandra – he had helped her invalid son – he surrounded himself with mistresses and corrupt officials, and was finally murdered in 1916 by poisoning, shooting and drowning.

Mansell Collection

Frank Spooner Pictures GAMMA

The Ku Klux Klan

The Klan was started in Tennessee, after the American Civil War. Members rode round the countryside disguised as the ghosts of soldiers, terrorizing the newly freed slaves. It was officially – but ineffectually – disbanded in 1871.

Mary Evans Picture Library

Stanley finds Livingstone

David Livingstone began his journey to find the source of the Nile in 1866, aged 53. His expedition was attacked and many members deserted; Livingstone was lost in Central Africa. In 1871 he was found by the journalist Henry Stanley, who saved his life.

Prussia, the Junkers, already assert that the turn of England will come next', one writer declared. And Queen Victoria's family links with Prussia made her increasingly unpopular as fears of a German invasion grew.

ATTACKS ON QUEEN VICTORIA

The Battle of Dorking, a fictitious narrative of a German conquest of England, had an enormous success in May. In June a German newspaper published an article suggesting that England was decadent and should agree to be ruled by Germany. This naturally added fuel to the fears of a German attack and anti-German and anti-monarchical feeling reached fever pitch. A republican group was formed within the ruling Liberal party

and its leader, Sir Charles Dilke, toured around the country making fiery speeches on behalf of the cause to huge and delighted audiences.

But at the year's end, the Prince of Wales fell seriously ill. Suddenly, almost miraculously, public opinion swung back on the side of the monarchy. 'The republicans say their chances are up,' wrote the Queen's cousin, the Duke of Cambridge. 'Heaven has sent this dispensation to save us.' *The Times* talked of divine intervention, of a whole nation regenerated by dint of prayer. It noted that other countries were following England's example, with even the French republicans being shamed into 'surprise and respect' for the Queen. Perhaps God, like the old order, was taking up the challenge flung down by all the revolutionaries and showing his strength.

Bulloz

Otto von Bismarck
The statesman Bismarck, seen here as a bloodthirsty butcher, was the mastermind of Germany's rise to power in Europe. His greatest moment came in January 1871, when France finally surrendered. The victory had made Bismarck the hero of the German people and he was created a prince. He then embarked on a policy of reform which made Germany the most modern and liberal – but not the most democratic – of European states.

Mary Evans Picture Library

Sir John Tenniel/Alice and Humpty Dumpty

Through the Looking Glass
As the eldest in a family of eight, Lewis Carroll learned early how to keep children amused – a talent he manifested in Alice's Adventures in Wonderland (1865) *and* Through the Looking Glass (1871), *tales told to Alice Liddell, a friend's daughter.*

GALLERY GUIDE

Note In December 1986 the Musée d'Orsay was opened in Paris, assembling under one roof a comprehensive collection of late-19th and early-20th century art, beginning from the year 1848, a time of change not only in art, but also in the social, economic and political spheres. Converted from an old railway station on the left bank of the Seine, the museum incorporates the Impressionist collection previously held in the Jeu de Paume; within the broad panorama offered by the museum, the full influence and importance of the Impressionist movement can be clearly seen.

Manet
The richest collection of Manet's pictures is to be found in Paris. The Musée d'Orsay contains most of the major early works, including The Luncheon on the Grass *(pp.24-5),* Olympia *(pp.26-7),* The Fifer *(p.28) and the* Balcony *(p.31). The Musée des Beaux-Arts in Tournai owns two fine specimens of his Impressionist style, while* The Grand Canal in Venice *is owned by the Provident Securities Co., San Francisco and* Boating *(pp.20-21) by the Metropolitan Museum of Art, New York. In London, the Courtauld Institute owns* A Bar at the Folies-Bergère *(p.33) and the National Gallery possesses his portrait of Eva Gonzalès. In America, Manet's Spanish style is well represented, most notably with* The Guitarrero *(Metropolitan Museum of Art, New York) and* The Dead Toreador *(National Gallery of Art, Washington).*

Degas
The best collection of Degas' popular ballet scenes is in Paris – most notably The Dancing Class *(p.61) and* The Ballet Rehearsal Room at the Opéra. *The* Ballet Rehearsal on Stage *(Metropolitan Museum of Art, New York) is one of his finest pastels. Two of Degas' equestrian paintings can be found in Boston:* Racehorses at Longchamp *(pp.58-9) and* Carriage at the Races *(p.47) (both in the Museum of Fine Arts). The Musée d'Orsay contains his best portrayals of the seamier side of life – for example,* Absinthe *(p.62) – while* The Milliner's Shop *(the Art Institute, Chicago) illustrates a more fashionable aspect of Paris. Degas' exotic paintings,* Miss Lala at the Cirque Fernando *and* Mme Camus with a Japanese Screen, *are both held by the National Gallery of Art, Washington.*

Monet
The most comprehensive collection of Monet's work is to be found in Paris. The Musée d'Orsay holds Rouen Cathedral *(p.95) and* Wild Poppies *(pp.88-9), and the Musée Marmottan, owns* Impression: Sunrise *(p.79). Also in Paris, at the Orangerie, is the most spectacular of the water-lily series. The Museum of Fine Arts in Boston owns* Snow at Argenteuil *and the portrait of* Madame Monet in Japanese Costume. *Further works can be found in Chicago and New York.*

Renoir
Renoir's Luncheon of the Boating Party *(pp.124-5) is in the Phillips Collection, Washington; that city is also the home of* The Odalisque *(p.109) and* The Girl with a Watering Can, *which are both in the National Gallery of Art, Washington). The late acceptance of Renoir's work in Europe has ensured the richness of many American collections.* The Bathers *(p.114) is at the Philadelphia Museum of Art, while* The Dance at Bougival *is in the Museum of Fine Arts, Boston. In Paris, the many notable examples of his work include* Le Moulin de la Galette *(pp.114-15) and* At the Piano *(both in the Musée d'Orsay).*

BIBLIOGRAPHY

G. Bazin, *French Impressionists in the Louvre*, Abrams, New York, 1958

J. Bouret, *Degas*, Thames & Hudson, London, 1965

F. Cachin and C. F. Moffett, *Manet, 1832-83*, Abrams, New York, 1984

F. Daulte, *Renoir*, Thames & Hudson, London, 1973

I. Dunlop, *Degas*, Harper & Row, New York, 1979

W. Gaunt, *The Impressionists*, Thames & Hudson, London, 1970

W. Gaunt, *Renoir*, Merrimack Pub. Circ., Topsfield, 1983

A. C. Hanson, *Manet and the Modern Tradition*, Yale University Press, New Haven, 1977

A. C. Hanson, *Renoir*, Abrams, New York, 1985

J. House, *Monet*, Phaidon, Oxford, 1981

J. Isaacson, *Claude Monet*, Phaidon, Oxford, 1978

P. Pool, *Impressionism*, Thames & Hudson, London, 1967

Jean Renoir, *Renoir, my Father*, Collins, London 1962

J. Rewald, *The History of Impressionism*, Museum of Modern Art, New York, 1961

J. Richardson, *Manet*, Phaidon, Oxford, 1967

W. C. Seitz, *Monet*, Abrams, New York, 1960

Frédéric Bazille (1841-70)

Born in Montpellier, Bazille came to Paris in 1862. There he failed his medical exams and entered Gleyre's studio, where his fellow-students included Monet, Sisley and Renoir. Like them, he admired the work of Manet and Courbet and, with Monet, he pioneered the idea of painting out-of-doors. The group portrait of his family (1867, Musée d'Orsay, Paris) is his finest achievement in this direction. Bazille's early death – he was killed in the Franco-Prussian War – prevented him from capitalizing on his early experiments in Impressionism.

Eugène Boudin (1824-98)

One of the founding fathers of Impressionism. Born at Honfleur, the son of a ship's captain, Boudin worked initially in a framing shop before devoting himself to painting. He set up an art centre at the Ferme Saint-Siméon, where he encouraged his fellow artists to experiment with open-air painting. Jongkind, Bazille and Monet were among those who joined the group and the latter in particular was deeply influenced by Boudin's atmospheric beach and harbour scenes. His favourite locations were the Normandy resorts of Deauville and Trouville, although the fashionable promenading figures were usually dwarfed by vast expanses of breezy or cloudy sky. Boudin contributed to the first Impressionist exhibition in 1874, but remained unaffected by the later developments of the movement.

Gustave Caillebotte (1848-94)

A talented amateur painter, chiefly remembered for his patronage of the Impressionists. Caillebotte was a friend of both Monet and Renoir. His style echoed that of the former (Sailing Boats at Argenteuil in the Musée d'Orsay, Paris, is a fine example) and he figured prominently in the latter's Luncheon of the Boating Party *(pp.124-5); Gustave is seated in the foreground. Caillebotte organized and appeared in several of the Impressionist exhibitions. His collection of paintings was bequeathed to the State and it formed the basis of the Jeu de Paume Museum. The collection has now been transferred to the Musée d'Orsay.*

Mary Cassatt (1845-1926)

The daughter of a wealthy American banker, Cassatt was born in Pittsburgh and travelled extensively throughout Europe in her youth. In 1866 she settled in Paris where she studied under the academic painter, Chaplin. However, she felt a greater affinity for the work of Courbet, Monet and Degas and it was the latter who invited her to exhibit with the Impressionists, after seeing her portrait of Zola at the 1874 Salon. Cassatt contributed to four of their shows (1879, 1880, 1881, 1886) and helped popularize the style in the United States. Her firm draughtsmanship and her ability to capture precise gestures were reminiscent of Degas, although she lacked his sense of cool detachment. She preferred to paint women and the Girl arranging her Hair (National Gallery of Art, Washington) is a fine example of her intimist technique.

Jean-Baptiste-Camille Corot (1796-1875)

French landscape painter and a major forerunner of the Impressionist movement. After a classical education, Corot travelled to Italy in 1825, where he developed his distinctive treatment of light, based on an understanding of tonal values rather than on pure draughtsmanship. His early unaffected works, for the most part composed in the open air, were more important for the Impressionists than the misty and poetic scenes, harking back to the

Berthe Morisot

(right) The first woman to join the Impressionist group, Berthe Morisot met Manet in 1868. He painted this portrait in 1872 when Morisot was 31 years old.

La Place du Théâtre Français

(far right) Pissarro here tries to capture the impression of movement in a busy street; by taking a high viewpoint and blurring the figures, his painting resembles a photograph.

Manet: Berthe Morisot with a Bunch of Violets

Lauros-Giraudon/Private Collection

Mr and Mrs George Gard de Sylva Collection/Los Angeles County Museum of Art

tradition of Claude, which made his reputation in the Salons. Corot remained an adventurous painter, however, and his later studies of women owed much to the example of Courbet and Manet.

Charles Gleyre (1808-74)
Swiss-born painter who settled in Paris in 1838. Gleyre's academic style earned him some success at the Salon, but it was his teaching that was important to the Impressionists. At his studio in the Ecole des Beaux-Arts, he taught Monet, Renoir, Sisley and Bazille, encouraging them in the practice of plein air painting.

Eva Gonzalès (1849-83)
French painter, daughter of the novelist Emmanuel Gonzalès. Eva studied initially under Brion but her style was formed by Manet, her second master. Her favourite subjects were scenes of contemporary Parisian society (The Box at the Théâtre des Italiens in the Musée d'Orsay is a notable example), painted with the dark tones and clear outlines that were typical of Manet's early pictures. After 1870, she turned increasingly to pastels, producing some of her finest work. Gonzalès' death in 1883 followed closely upon Manet's.

Armand Guillaumin (1841-1927)
French landscape painter, associated with the Impressionists. Guillaumin attended the Académie Suisse in Paris, where he met Cézanne and Pissarro. He exhibited at the Salon des Refusés and also contributed to six of the eight Impressionist shows. However, his career was frequently hampered by lack of money – he worked for the railways until 1868 and was not financially independent until he won a lottery in 1891. Guillaumin's early style was modelled on Pissarro, although his colours became increasingly vivid. In common with the Neo-Impressionists, he was fond of depicting industrial subjects.

Johan Barthold Jongkind (1819-91)
A Dutch marine and landscape painter, one of the most important precursors of the Impressionist movement. Jongkind trained at the Hague, but spent most of his life in France. In 1862, he stayed at Le Havre, where he met Boudin and started sketching in water-colour out of doors. His delicate, broken brushwork and his sensitive atmospheric effects influenced both Boudin and the young Monet. Jongkind's career was punctuated by frequent bouts of alcoholism and mental instability, and at the end of his life he was confined to an asylum in Grenoble.

Berthe Morisot (1841-95)
The first woman to join the Impressionist group. Morisot was the daughter of the Prefect of Bourges, but moved to Paris in 1852. She knew Fantin-Latour and Corot and her early work owed much to the encouragement of the latter. In 1868, she met Manet and eventually married his brother in 1874. Morisot appeared in a number of Manet's pictures and helped persuade him to take up plein air painting. She exhibited at all but one of the Impressionist shows, specializing in quiet, domestic scenes. In later years, her style was increasingly influenced by the art of Renoir.

Camille Pissarro (1830-1903)
A leading figure in the Impressionist movement. Born on the island of St Thomas in the West Indies, he worked initially in his father's store before running off to paint in Venezuela. Reluctantly, his family accepted his artistic ambitions and sent him to Paris in 1855. There, his early work bore the stamp of Corot's and Courbet's influence. In 1859, he met Monet at the Académie Suisse and soon adopted the practice of plein air painting. However, while Monet specialized in fleeting atmospheric effects, Pissarro evinced a preference for more solid landscapes and, in particular, for rustic villages and country lanes. He exhibited both at the Salon and the Salon des Refusés, but the Franco-Prussian War proved a disastrous setback to his career. After he fled to London, the German army turned his house into a butcher's shop, destroying most of his large stock of canvases. Upon his return, he settled in Pontoise, where Cézanne, among others, came to learn from him. Pissarro was a lifelong socialist and an unfailing supporter of the Impressionist movement. He was the only artist to exhibit at all eight of the Impressionist shows and his conciliatory nature was often called upon to quell the many divisions within the group. Pissarro was also the most experimental of the Impressionists. For five years (c.1885-90), he worked in the Pointillist style devised by Seurat, and he also pioneered the depiction of bustling street scenes. In later years, his failing eyesight forced him to abandon open-air painting, but his output remained prodigious.

Lucien Pissarro (1863-1944)
Eldest son of Camille Pissarro. Lucien's style followed that of his father, displaying both Impressionist and Pointillist features. In 1890 he moved to London, where he played a part in the Arts and Crafts movement, and in 1896 he founded the Eragny Press.

Alfred Sisley (1839-99)
French Impressionist, born in Paris but of English parentage. In 1856, his father sent him to England to train for a commercial career, but Sisley soon abandoned this for painting, and in 1862 he entered Gleyre's studio. There, he met Monet, Renoir and Bazille and worked with them in the region of Fontainebleau and the Seine. He exhibited at the Salon des Refusés (1863) and at the first Impressionist exhibition (1874), and also contributed to the latter's subsequent shows in 1876, 1877 and 1882. Apart from several brief spells in England, Sisley worked exclusively in northern France, where he developed a sensitive landscape style similar to Monet's, and excelled at the creation of water, snow and mist effects.

Philip Wilson Steer (1860-1942)
British painter, the most notable of the English Impressionists. Steer studied in Paris, at the Académie Jullian and the Ecole des Beaux-Arts, where he drew on the influence of Whistler and Monet. Returning home, he exhibited at the New English Art Club, of which he was a co-founder, and at the London Impressionist exhibition (1889) organized by Sickert. Steer's most engaging works were his sunny beach scenes, which are reminiscent of Monet and the Neo-Impressionists. Later, he reverted to a landscape style based on that of Constable and Turner.

INDEX

WITHDRAWAL